The
STONE BOUDOIR

ALSO BY
THERESA MAGGIO

Mattanza: Love and Death in the
Sea of Sicily

The
STONE BOUDOIR

*Travels Through the
Hidden Villages of
Sicily*

THERESA MAGGIO

PERSEUS
PUBLISHING

A Member of the Perseus Books Group

These stories are true but some names have been changed to protect privacy.
"Roccella Valdèmone" is from the November–December 1999 issue of *Islands*. Copyright © 1997 by Islands Publishing Co. Reprinted by permission.

Library of Congress Control Number: 2001098258
ISBN 0-7382-0342-4

Perseus Publishing is a member of the Perseus Books Group.
Find us on the World Wide Web at http://www.perseuspublishing.com
Perseus Publishing books are available at special discounts for bulk purchases in the U.S. by corporations, institutions, and other organizations. For more information, please contact the Special Markets Department at the Perseus Books Group, 11 Cambridge Center, Cambridge, MA 02142, or call (800)255-1514 or (617)252-5298, or e-mail j.mccrary@perseusbooks.com.

Text design by Deborah Gayle
Set in 11-point Goudy by Perseus Publishing Services

First printing, March 2002

1 2 3 4 5 6 7 8 9 10—04 03 02

To the memory of my sister,
SUSAN

CONTENTS

Contents

ACKNOWLEDGEMENTS

My thanks to those who helped me on my way: Natalie Oana and Jeannin, Brigitte, and Enzo Russo; Piero Corrao; Nella Cartafalsa; Palmina La Rosa and her family; my hill gang—Jackie and Nicholas Toth, Joan and David Spikol, Andy Yablonsky, and Margaret Stearns, for all the nourishment, warmth, and inspiration; A. Pierce Haviland; Archer Mayor; Andy Zito, guitar; Jo Cella for the angels; Professore Michele LoMonaco, for teaching me Italian; Perseus Books, for sticking with me; Eleonora Consoli; Totò Podestà and his mother, Francesca; Melissa and Michael Theil; Kate Scott, copy editor; Enza Dolce; Giuseppina Dolce; Cristina and Giovanni La Rosa; Rosaria and Antonietta Riccobene; Stacey Toth; Valentina Bua; Andrea Sweatt Emmons; Michael Aiello; Eugenio Strano; Adriana Strano; Marta M. Lotti; Luisa Amendolia; Carmelo and Nella Bua; Santo Lipani; Graziella Ortolano; Mary Kay Hartley; Joan Tapper; Sally and Upton Brady; librarians everywhere; Amanda Cook, my wonderful editor; and all who wished me well.

Acknowledgements

My special thanks to my sisters, Dorothy and Marion; to my father, Joseph A. Maggio; to Aunt Freda Maggio, who passed away while I wrote; and to Nana and Papa, who are always with me.

PREFACE

SOMETHING THRUMS IN THE STONES of Sicilian hill towns, and I have become obsessed with them.

About a dozen years ago I saw the film *L'Uomo delle Stelle* (*The Star Maker*) directed by Giuseppe Tornatore, a Sicilian from Bagheria, who had also made my favorite movie, the Oscar-winning *Nuovo Cinema Paradiso*. Set in the 1950's, *The Star Maker* was about a con man from Rome who drove to Sicilian mountain towns in a painted truck charging people for screen tests he conducted with no film in his camera. Peasants paid their last lire to pour their hearts out to his lens.

I paid little attention to the plot because I was gaping at the real towns where the film was shot. They were simple stone villages, nothing spectacular, but so appealing, set high inside the island where you don't see the sea. They called to me from the screen. Later I rented the film so I could write down the towns' names as they rolled by in the final credits. Then I stowed the list in a safe place. Someday I would go to these villages.

Years later, in 1992, I finally had enough time and money to carry out my plan, and I flew to Sicily. But I forgot the list! I couldn't remember the villages' names. I headed inland to the mountains and left my destinations to serendipity, stopping at towns in northwest-central Sicily and on Mount Etna's slopes. I went to fill my eye, and I always got an earful as a bonus.

A couple of weeks ago, some of my sister's Sicilian friends came to visit and brought *The Star Maker* videotape with them. This time I followed the plot. Early on, Giò, the charlatan "star maker," ravishes Beata, a starry-eyed virgin raised in a country convent; the girl clings to Giò, whom she sees as her ticket out of misery. Unaware that the camera is empty, she travels with him from town to town and unwittingly helps him to defraud her own kind as they squander their poignant tales on an empty box.

Giò gives the townspeople lines from *Gone with the Wind* to recite, but many cannot read, so some just talk about what is on their minds. A shepherd tells the camera he doesn't know what the stars are. Mafiosi require Giò to film their boss's wake. A politician uses his screen test as a soapbox. A *carabiniere* stops Giò's truck because he wants to recite his Sicilian translation of the *Inferno* before the camera. Cave-dwelling bandits nearly kill Giò, but he buys his life with another phony test. A desperate mother pays for her daughter's test with sex in the cab of Giò's truck.

As Giò drives through this hermetic, alien world of the interior, he swears to himself that all Sicilians must be crazy.

Born on the continent, he cannot penetrate the thick layers of diverse civilizations, religions, languages, conquerors, of heartache and blood, that made the islanders the way they are. Sicily peels like an onion, and few have seen its core. When Giò's ruse is revealed, he goes to jail, and the beauty he has deflowered goes mad. I see Beata's betrayal as Tornatore's metaphor for the rape of Sicily, an alluring island whose fertile land and strategic position have always brought power and gain to invaders. The relationship between the con man and the convent girl was just the filmmaker's excuse to tell the tales and frame the faces and mountains of his beloved island, where nothing is as it seems.

At the end of the tape I watched in amazement as the towns' names scrolled by—Polizzi Generosa, Geraci Siculo, Alimena, Petralia, Blufi, Locati, and San Mauro. I had been to all of them and more, without my list, drawn by luck, intuition, or the sound of their names. This collection of stories was my excuse to explore my obsession with the stones and to understand the island my grandparents left. Sicily is a mysterious, overpowering attraction, like love or a drug. I arrived in the mountain towns by bus or by train with a notebook in my knapsack and set off with my Pentax loaded.

The
STONE BOUDOIR

I

CIOLINO

߷

I WAS ON A MISSION: to find the smallest mountain towns in Sicily. Tiny jewels, remote and isolated, these are places tourists seldom see. But they are the island's hidden treasure and the secret spring of Sicilian endurance.

One town led to another. I'd stare at my map, now flannel-soft at the edges, and look for a small dot with an appealing name. Then I'd get on a bus and go. That's how I came to Polizzi Generosa, a town of four thousand people teetering on a peak in the Madonie Mountains in north-central Sicily, a quiet world of mist and moss on old stones.

I liked Polizzi so much that I rented an apartment there for two weeks. One day I explained my search to Signora Riccobene, the grocer. "If you're looking for a small town," she said, "you must go to Locati." Her twin daughters, both pharmacists, owned a drugstore there. I checked my map; Locati didn't rate a dot. My kind of town. If I wanted to go, all I had to do was meet Antonietta and Rosaria at six the next morning, and they would drive me there.

For several days I made their pharmacy my base camp. There I met the black-shawled women and men bent over canes who came in to have their prescriptions filled. One thousand people lived in Locati, and soon only the old would be left; the young leave for school and desk jobs in the city. No one wants to be a farmer anymore.

Rosaria and Antonietta were kind to their aged customers and always listened to their sorrows. Seventy-year-old Signora Maria, a regular, had lived most of her life alone in a thatched stone hut in a village much smaller than Locati. A stroke had forced her to move to town three years before, but she still longed for her abandoned home in the wheatfields of Ciolino.

One afternoon the sisters planned a surprise. They closed up shop, picked up Signora Maria, and drove us to her old home. The summer landscape slid by under a matte, blue sky—tawny fields of wheat, fresh furrows of earth, the rustling gray-green crowns of olive trees. Signora Maria hadn't seen her cottage since she locked its door and left it. Slight, with blue eyes and gray hair, she stared out at the land and told us her life.

She had never married. A peasant farmer's only child, she lived with her parents on a dirt road in the middle of wide wheatfields. Her family was too poor to own a car, so when they needed supplies, her father took Maria on the donkey and walked to Locati, the closest town with stores. They had to wade across the river because there was no bridge. "It was all mud," she said. "When it rained, you couldn't walk."

Her father died when she was seven, leaving only the house and the donkey. Maria was heartbroken when her mother sold the beast and they waded one last time across the river to Locati, where there might be work. For the next two years, Maria's mother had heart trouble. Then she died, and Maria was alone. She walked back to Ciolino and raised herself in the thatched stone hut.

"I worked in the wheat harvest. They used to sing," she said as we wound past orchards of almonds and pears. Maria gleaned the fields, the miller ground her grain, and she baked round loaves in the communal domed brick oven at the end of her street. To give Maria a trade, a kindly woman taught her how to give injections painlessly. People paid her with pasta, bread, and sacks of grain. "We all respected one another," she said.

There were seventy families in her village then. At *Carnevale*, before Lent, they would dance until dawn. But Maria spent most of her time alone, cooking, baking, sewing, cleaning, and washing for one. "You were a little girl," I said. "Did you ever have time for fun?" She did; in her spare time she memorized long folk poems. Once learned, a poem was hers forever, the one thing that couldn't be taken from her.

She was quiet a moment, then the words bubbled up from sixty years before, and Signora Maria began to recite a folk epic in rhymed, rhythmic quatrains. It told of heroes and villains and women in love, a story about courage and poverty, true friends and betrayal. She recited for ten minutes, as if in a trance, using stage whispers and shouts that once would have lured her neighbors to gather and listen.

The sign at the turn for Ciolino said: "Beyond this point the streets have no names." And as far as we could see, no trees and no houses, only the sinewy ripple of wheat stalks, plush as puma fur, in fields vast and golden. Now only twenty families remained, Signora Maria said.

Her old neighbors, who knew we were coming, met us at the door of the square stone house they had built and roofed with red tiles. They had abandoned their traditional straw-thatched hut years before for the conveniences of modern living. Signora Maria stepped out of the car and looked worriedly at her old house next door. It seemed to have sprouted from the ground and now was going back to it. The straw roof, once stiff as a broom, was bowed and rotting. When it buckled, the world it once sheltered, her girlhood, would be gone forever. Our hostess put her arm around Maria and led us into her own house to a trestle table laden with crusty bread, homemade cheese, plates of sliced mortadella, and bowls of black olives. Her husband, a farmer, opened a door off the dining room, flung his arm wide, and showed us his treasure: a storeroom stacked to the ceiling with plump burlap sacks of hard Sicilian durum.

Signora Maria ate little but waited politely until the table was cleared. Then she fished a skeleton key from her purse, walked to her cottage, pushed open the door, and stepped in.

The only light came through the cracks in the thatching. It was a single large room whose beamed ceiling came to a point high above its center. The beams rose from limestone-block walls built to chest level. The floor was smoothed cement. The rest of the house was of straw.

The neighbors, their son, the twins, and I traipsed about in this relic of another time. I lay on the floor and took pictures of the roof beams, then walked around taking notes. No one thought to leave Maria alone with her memories.

The house was as she had left it. Her bed was against the wall opposite the door, a quilt still folded at its foot. A broom leaned against the wall. Wooden vegetable crates had been her chest of drawers, a bedside table her only real furniture. A curtain on a clothesline divided the room. Her eyes followed a sunbeam up to the roof.

"When it rained, it never leaked," she said.

She led us to the outdoor kitchen she had built with her own hands—two stone walls with a tiled roof and an iron pot hung over a fire pit. Signora Maria had lived here without electricity or plumbing. There was the galvanized bucket she had used to haul water from the well; the tall terra-cotta amphora she had filled with oil, its pointed bottom snugged in a sand bed, as it would have been on a Phoenician trading ship; the white enameled bowl where she had bathed; the shard of mirror before which she had combed her hair; the fingernail brush on a hook. Niches carved in the wall were her dish drainers. A caned wooden chair, covered with cobwebs, was set in a corner.

Signora Maria was on her knees, searching with a broom handle for something under the bed.

With the broomstick she pulled out a brown leather book bag. She stood up, wiped the dust from it with her sleeve, and hugged it. She would not say what she thought was in it, and she would not open it before us.

A few days later I called the twins from a phone booth in Sperlinga, where some people still live in cave homes in a cliff. Rosaria answered the phone.

"What was in the book bag?" I asked.

"The poems," she said.

2

NANA AND PAPA

WHENEVER I FLY INTO PALERMO, the plane circles and dips over the powder-blue sea and I see the two-man fishing boats with their nets streaming like lace ribbons behind them. Low clouds cling like cherubim to the sides of Monte Pellegrino. The passengers always applaud when we touch ground. After they have been away for a while, Sicilians are as happy to be back on their island as I am.

Maybe I am so drawn to Sicily because I am half Sicilian and the island is hard-wired into my genes. Or maybe Sicily is a vortex that pulls some people in—a center of the universe, like the Omphalos at Delphi, a navel stone that connected some inner world to the outer. Here the bedrock hums with hidden energy. Sicilians use it to build their houses, churches, and streets. Their lives saturate the rock, carving niches, and pooling in the voids. Like water, the people taste of the stone that contains them. Sicily is a hard place to leave.

My father's parents emigrated from Santa Margherita Belice, in the mountains south of Palermo, at the beginning of the twentieth century. When she was twelve years old, Alfonsa Adamo said goodbye to her mother and younger sisters and left the island to live with relatives in Brooklyn. There, Giuseppe Maggio, her future husband, had rooms in the same building.

Papa, my grandfather, had red hair and china-blue eyes set in a pear-shaped face, but I knew him when his hair was white and he walked with crutches. He was a short, solid, stocky *contadino*, which means both peasant and farmer. Every fall he would weave a reed blanket for the fig tree so it wouldn't freeze in the northeastern winter. He made paper corn stalks and funny hats for my sisters and me from the comics section of the *Daily News* and always kept quarters for grandchildren under the kitchen tablecloth. He never learned to read or write his own language and I don't remember him speaking English, and he taught me to play checkers by never letting me win.

Nana was dark and strong and she was the real head of the family. In Santa Margherita she had attended a convent school where the nuns taught her sewing and how to speak and write proper Italian. Her mother ran a store where she sold bridal trousseaux, the cutwork sheets and fancy linens that a Margheritese bride brings to her marriage—sheets and blankets for six winter beds and six sets for summer. Nana's father was an overseer, a *sovrastante*, for a baron; his job was to weigh the grain and cheese with which peasants paid their taxes.

In New York, Papa got a job as a garbage collector for the city. One day at the dump he kicked a brown paper bag and a dead baby rolled out. He was horrified, but said nothing, fearing he would be blamed, and he quit that day. Later he worked for the railroad and in restaurant kitchens. Alfonsa and Giuseppe's first child was born in Brooklyn; then Nana and Papa moved to the country, to the New Jersey Meadowlands, so they could have a garden and a grapevine. That's where my father was born. Papa worked nights in New Jersey, and Nana commuted to New York City's garment district all week and in the evenings and on weekends sewed sequins on gowns at home. She bought tickets to matinée performances of the Metropolitan Opera and taught herself English by reading the *New York Times* aloud. By day, Papa tended their five children, their chickens, the kitchen garden, and the grapevine.

When I was growing up in Carlstadt, my family spent every Sunday after church at Nana's house. In summer our Sicilian relatives would come from Brooklyn to sit in the shade and smell the frosty blue grapes under Papa's arbor. The Jersey sun filtered through the broad green leaves and we tuned out the hum of the traffic whizzing behind us on Route 17. The men sat on Depression-green benches at a picnic table and played checkers while they waited for the women to bring food: plates of artichokes and dried tomatoes in oil, crunchy green fennel, and cold cuts. Then pasta with meat sauce in a broad hand-painted bowl, then barbecued chicken and sausages my grandmother made with meat she required the butcher to grind before her eyes. Then came the walnuts, plums, and cherries, and cookies from the Italian pastry shop. Papa sat up straight and gripped his fly swatter like a scepter. He'd whack the table, then hold up a flattened fly by the wing. He never missed.

The aunts and uncles brought our innumerable cousins. We, the children, mainstreamed Americans, spoke no Italian, but the grown-ups used Sundays to be Sicilian together. They spoke in the deep dialect peculiar to Santa Margherita for the pleasure of it—it affirmed their common bond—and to keep secrets from the kids. Years later, when I asked my Aunt Freda what they would talk about, she said, "It was always Santa Margherita," that hill town they had escaped yet still longed for.

As I got older, I realized that Sundays weren't like this for everybody. My friends called their grandmothers Grandma. Their grandparents didn't speak in broken English, didn't make such a ritual of a meal. By the time I was eight, I understood that this was a Sicilian thing, but I didn't know what Sicily was. Nana showed me a map of a three-cornered island being booted toward the Strait of Gibraltar. She said it was once part of the Kingdom of the Two Sicilies. "When I was a girl, a princess used to wave to me from her balcony when I walked my donkey through town," she said. To tell you the truth, I didn't believe her, even though Nana was not the type to tell fairy tales.

When I was fifteen and Nana was in her seventies, I sat on a stool in her basement kitchen and watched her stir a vat of sauce. Papa had parboiled the tomatoes and pushed them through a hand-cranked crusher clamped to the edge of the table. Now she added a few basil leaves to the pot. Her back was to me.

She could have bought a plane ticket to Sicily if she had wanted to. She and Papa had bought three houses in northern New Jersey and helped four sons start businesses, marry, and build homes. "Nana," I asked, "why, in all these years, have you never gone back?" She wheeled around and spat the words at me.

"There's nothing there," was all she said.

To her, Sicily meant Santa Margherita, and an earthquake had destroyed it while she was living in New Jersey. She'd never seen the rest of the island, except when she was twelve and was on her farewell trip from the mountains to Palermo, where she boarded a ship that took her to Naples, and then to New York. On the night from the fourteenth to the fifteenth of January 1968, an earthquake crumbled most of Santa Margherita and all or part of nine other hill towns. In a sense, there really was nothing left there. Nana spoke no more to me about Sicily. The subject was taboo; I came to think of Sicily as the family's skeleton in the closet.

Papa died of a heart attack a year after the earthquake. Twenty years later, Nana died too. Among her papers I found a letter her cousin Betta had written to her five weeks after the earthquake. "We are living in tents because the house is uninhabitable. Nothing to eat until today. We still feel tremors from time to time, no one knows when they are supposed to end. We live as God wills."

Nobody told me what my grandparents escaped when they left Sicily near the turn of the twentieth century—the poverty and corruption, wheat failures and famine, drought, the latrines in the stone stables, the rule of the Mafia, the roaming bands of dogs who would take over the village after dark. The Sicily Nana and Papa left was a place where ordinary people could work hard and never get ahead. Bribes, threats, protection money, and high taxes sapped their savings and their souls. So they came to America and did not discuss Sicily with the children. The day Nana told me there was nothing there I decided that I would see Sicily for myself.

When I was a college junior majoring in French and spending a semester in Paris, I kept that promise. It was 1973. I had ten days between the end of spring term and a summer job as an au pair. I bought a train ticket through to Palermo, and a textbook, *L'Italien sans peine*, from a Seine bookstall, and set out for Sicily. By the time we reached Rome, I had memorized how to ask, "From which track does the train leave?" and "Where is the bathroom?" I got by on that, my French, my Catholic-school Latin, and sign language. South of Rome, I saw no other women on the train.

The crowded cars clacked south all night. I was in a second-class compartment with five men, all with stubble beards, all sleeping sitting up. Pasquale boarded in Naples, and the compartment woke up as he settled in. Then Pasquale opened his wallet and showed us all the beauty of Rosalia, his *fidanzata,* who lived on the outskirts of Palermo. At three in the morning the train reached the Strait of Messina, at the tip of the Italian boot. At land's end, where the train breaks up into sections to drive onto a ferry, the oldest man in the compartment woke me up. He led me up on deck and pointed to the moon, nearly full, reflected on the glassy black sea. The last lights of land twinkled behind us as we crossed between Scylla and Charybdis. The statue of the Madonna blessed the mainland harbor as she had blessed the Sicilian diaspora a hundred years before, when millions of southern Italians were leaving, maybe forever, the little towns that had spawned them, the only place they had ever known. The inscription on her pedestal reads BENEDICIMUS VOS ET CIVITAS VOSTRA—"We bless you and your town."

The lights of Messina grew brighter. Half an hour later we reached the Sicilian shore. The train cars linked up again, stretched out, and picked up speed for the last leg along the north coast. Cefalù, Termini, Torre Normanna. Dawn broke; the waters of the Tyrrhenian Sea lapped the sand near the tracks. We were coming into Palermo.

With sign language my fellow travelers gave me my instructions: Put your passport in your bra, carry your purse with its latch against your body, and watch out for thieves (a finger to the eye, a rippling of the fingers). I was intending to catch the daily bus to Santa Margherita, but the bus wasn't there. I was already a day late because I hadn't realized the train ride took two days and two nights from Paris. There was no other public transportation to my ancestral village. I couldn't afford a taxi and I decided not to hitchhike. I didn't even know where Santa Margherita was; I couldn't find it on my map. Now I was scared. So I plunked my bags at a table out-side the station café, felt for my passport in my bra, ordered a cappuccino, and told myself not to worry. I just had to think.

Pasquale, the one with the fiancée in Palermo, walked over to me. He pressed his thumb against four fingers and wagged his hand under his chin. "What are you doing here?" I shrugged. Even if I had known, I couldn't have explained it. He pawed the air once, a sign for me to follow.

He went to a pay phone, called someone, and said he would be arriving with an *americana*. Neither of us could afford a taxi, so we lugged our heavy suitcases under the hot June sky to a housing project on the edge of the city. Uncollected garbage stewed in the sun. We stopped in front of a ground-floor apartment door, Pasquale pressed the buzzer, the door swung open, and two meaty, matronly arms embraced me, muffling my face between enormous breasts. I couldn't breathe.

It was his fiancée's mother. She let me go and invited me in. Inside I met the fiancée, pretty as her picture, and her father. Rosalia's mother first served us coffee, then a glass of wine and a three-course dinner. I had no hope of understand-ing a word they said; they spoke in the Palermo dialect, but it felt familiar and comfortable. Two more hours went by and still I had heard no mention of the words "Santa Margherita." Their hospitality seemed so complete that I started to wonder whether I was now supposed to unpack and move in. I was twenty years old and pure American; I had to make something happen. So I stood up and announced in Italian, using verbs in their infinitive forms, that I would have to be going, thanks for dinner, very kind, but I must find my way, my relatives would be worried.

General commotion. They would not hear of this. It turned out that everybody was waiting for Cosimo, Rosalia's brother, to get home with the car. He would guard his sister's honor while the four of us—Cosimo, Rosalia, Pasquale, and I—drove to Santa Margherita. Cosimo came home, ate, then looked in the encyclopedia for my ancestral village. No one found it, but we all piled into his car anyway, for some reason confident that the town was on the western side of the island.

Guys in the front seat, girls in the back, we took the coast road and headed counterclockwise around Sicily in the late afternoon. The sea sparkled blue to our right. A breeze flickered the silvery leaves of the olive trees to our left. Cosimo was lost, but he hated to ask for directions; he didn't trust Sicilians. In Italy, if you ask directions of someone you don't know, and he doesn't know the way, you will never hear a simple "Sorry, I don't know." Why lose face to a stranger when you can give him detailed directions to someplace he never wanted to go instead?

So we pulled off the highway and found a priest. Cosimo rolled down the window and asked him the way. The priest gave us directions, Cosimo rolled up the window before the priest was done, saying "Sì, sì, sì," as if he didn't believe a word of it. He pulled over and parked. We all got out and went into a cool dark church, to pray for guidance I supposed. After that we wandered along the coast aimlessly for hours until we came to a road sign for Santa Margherita and turned inland toward the hills.

At eleven that night, we found the "temporary" barracks my relatives had occupied for the five years since the earthquake. Via Firenze, number 35. I got out of the car, stretched, and said, in English, "Thank God, we made it." The foreign words started an avalanche of relatives and curious neighbors who poured into the street. In 1973, the arrival of a member of the American branch of a family was still an event.

A short, bent little woman with her gray hair in a braid down her back, her face half hidden by a black kerchief, her eyes black and unseeing, scurried out into the street. This was Zia Betta, my Aunt Betta, Nana's first cousin and best friend who had written the letter telling about life in the tents right after the earthquake. Betta was my closest relative here. Behind Betta were her middle-aged daughter, Carmela, and Carmela's husband, Calogero. And Vito, Carmela's brother, with his wife and daughter. My family was a crowd unto itself. A warm yellow light fell from the window; they had been burning votive candles for me. They greeted my protectors with hugs and grateful kisses for fellow Sicilians who had done the right thing, taking me in tow like that. Cosimo turned down their invitation to a midnight meal of pasta and breaded veal cutlets, bit his lip when Calogero gave him directions back to the coast, and then the three of them left me alone with my Sicilian relatives.

Old Zia Betta gave me a stone amulet to pin to my shirt to ward off the Evil Eye while I was in town. "People are jealous," she explained. I smelled rain on the breeze; Calogero ushered me inside and warned me to kick away dogs during a thunderstorm because they attract lightning. Carmela turned down the bed we would share and removed a bouquet of flowers from the night table, because at night, flowers suck up all the oxygen.

I lay on my pillow between clean ironed sheets, staring into the black ceiling of the cramped little structure and thought to myself, *I am in Sicily, and there IS something here*.

3

ROCCELLA VALDÈMONE

❧

THAT WAS HOW IT STARTED. Soon I was hooked. This island was deadly beautiful, very old, most powerful and strange. I stayed away for eleven years after my first visit, but Sicily stayed inside me. I finished college, camped across Canada with friends, hitchhiked the States coast to coast a couple times, and learned to tend bar, a good traveling trade. I turned thirty in journalism school and vowed to put my degree to good use.

But the year after that I decided to take my father to see his parents' village. Dad wanted to stop first at Mondello, a seaside town near Palermo, where he had served in the U.S. Navy after World War Two. We liked it so much we stayed five days. Piero, the lifeguard at the tourist beach, was a fisherman the rest of the year. He and I fell in love in short order.

After several long vacations in Sicily, I moved to Mondello for a year in 1986. Piero paid for my Italian lessons with fish. In the winter I taught English in Palermo and wrote for a small local monthly paper. Piero and I lived one hundred yards from the sea. He fished Mondello Bay in his fifteen-foot wooden boat, the *Francesca*. I traveled around Sicily and took pictures.

I spent my money on film, so Piero bought me lunch every day at the Renato Bar, the hot-lunch bar closest to the sea. One day I had a stroke of luck.

A procession of elderly men and women filed by the seafront bar, their old faces with deep creases lifelong works of art framed by caps and kerchiefs. They were Sicilian, but they weren't from this seaside town. Theirs were the broad, open, country faces of farmers and their wives.

"Where are they from?" I asked Piero, as if he should know.

Piero shrugged. "*Carrapipi*," he said, Sicilian for Podunk.

The strangers filed into a restaurant, leaving me spellbound by their faces. I went home to get my camera, then waited for them in the square where their tour bus was parked.

Three hours later they emerged from the restaurant. They had arranged for a local photographer to take their picture, and suddenly they asked to have me in it. Twenty of the old ones pressed together in front of the mermaid fountain with me in their midst. They told me they were from Roccella Valdèmone, a tiny mountain town of a thousand people.

"Once a year, the town pays for a trip for the old people," said a middle-aged woman who was shepherding the group. "Otherwise they'd never get out of town." She opened her map and pointed to a dot on the other side of Sicily, halfway between the Ionian Sea and Mount Etna's peak. She invited me to visit. Before they left, I took some pictures of them.

In November, seven months later, I went unannounced to Roccella—two hours on a coach to Catania, then three hours up switchbacks in a jitney to the top of a mountain where the town had stood since at least the thirteenth century. I was the only passenger, and Roccella was the last stop. It was dark when the driver cut the motor. I asked him where I could find a *pensione* and a place to eat.

"There are no hotels or restaurants in this town," he said.

I had no one's name or address in Roccella, but I had my pictures. They were slides. I slid them one by one into my handheld viewer and showed them in the dark to the bus driver.

"That man works right here," he said, and he pointed to an auto repair shop.

The mechanic knew me instantly. He had been one of the guides on the old people's trip, and he acted as if he had been expecting me. He washed his hands, closed up shop, and walked me to the mayor's house, where he picked up the keys to the town hall. *Perhaps I am to sleep here,* I thought, but instead he opened the mayor's top desk drawer and handed me the photo they'd saved for months. There I was, nestled in with the old ones in front of the mermaid, the April sun on our faces.

Wet cobblestones glistened under the street lamps as we walked to a house where I would stay. There Signora Lombardo sat on a wooden chair set over a charcoal brazier, peeling potatoes for stew. The coals warmed her through the wicker seat. Her son, Carmelo, a music teacher at the high school, showed me to my room.

After supper I stopped in the piazza, where everyone already knew of my arrival. Three teenage boys invited me to be the guest deejay at their radio station. I sent greetings from America over the airwaves, and then I played Madonna's "Papa Don't Preach." One boy brought a silver tray of amaretto cordials from the café next door.

"All over this side of the volcano, kids in their beds are holding their radios to their ears, listening to you," the young station manager told me.

I stepped outside into the drizzle. The houses in the valley were already dark. Etna was invisible, a black mountain against a black, starless sky, but a muffled red glow pulsed over the crater, its inner fire reflected by low clouds.

Next morning the town was beautiful, its stones freshly washed and silver gray. A quiet parade passed below my window: a man on a mule, then a goat, a dog, and a goose, heading in a line for the town watering trough. Later I met a young woman, a university student home for the weekend, who walked me to the site of Roccella's seven-hundred-year-old castle, its stones now scattered on the ground.

After lunch her father drove me to see Roccella's famous almond tree. Said to be the first to flower in Sicily, it blossoms in January. And just before sunset a farmer and his wife brought me to a dizzying brink to look down on the Alcàntara River, a silver ribbon running through the abyss, where lemon and orange trees grew, with grapevines slung between them, in terraced orchards.

On Tuesday morning Carmelo dropped me at the train station on his way to work. I had stayed three days and still had all the money I came with. His mother wanted only my picture in exchange for my room and board. I had been adopted by a town so small that most Sicilians had never heard of it, an isolated pocket of humanity where the ancient custom of treating a stranger as an honored guest still thrives.

4

PRICKLY PEARS

༃

PIERO AND I EVENTUALLY BROKE UP. I went back to the States, to Vermont, the place I love best, to work at the *Brattleboro Reformer*. But I couldn't get Sicily out of my mind. Just before I quit the paper, the last day of 1991, I applied for my first credit card. Then I left a job I loved, cashed in my 401K, and bought a plane ticket. I quit work to travel and write; the gain was time, the loss was money. That's why I always went to Sicily in the winter, when flights were cheap. I'd made several trips in the 1980's, mostly to study the workings of an ancient tuna trap used off the coast of the island of Favignana, but Santa Margherita was the first mountain town I got to know intimately. In the winter of 1992 I went back to Santa Margherita and stayed with Nella Cartafalsa, the niece of the daughter of my grandmother's first cousin (all my blood ties here were that tenuous). Nella's invitation gave me a close look at the sequestered life of a provincial hill-town woman.

The earthquake had destroyed the house Nella's family rented, and now she lived in subsidized housing and paid less than five dollars a month in rent. She was forty-two, unemployed, and unmarried and was caring for her widowed Aunt Carmela. Nella's father, a shoemaker, had died, leaving her only his barrel shape. She ate a diet heavy in pasta, potatoes, bread, and olive oil. Her favorite snack was a dollop of fresh sheep's-milk ricotta mixed with sugar, lemon zest, and chocolate shavings squeezed between two sugar cookies—a Sicilian Oreo.

Except for pajama bottoms, Nella never wore pants. At home she wore Dr. Scholl's sandals and a straight skirt that hung a few inches above the tops of her knee-high stockings. On the coldest mornings she kept her pajama bottoms on under her skirt. For public appearances (Saturday market, Sunday Mass, religious festivals, doctor's appointments, or to vote) she favored cruel shoes and a white wool suit, her only break from hill-town mores. She should have been wearing black to mourn her dead parents, but she wouldn't. Nella was just three years older than I. She had been living with her parents since we met nineteen years before, until first her mother died, then her father. Nella had invited her aunt, Zia Carmela, who shook with Parkinson's disease, to come and live with her in this modern two-story apartment. Carmela spoke only a heavy deep dialect, in a breathy whisper. Her widow's pension supported them both, and now me.

They managed because Nella was frugal. Spartan. At meals she tore her paper napkin in two and put half away to

use later. She used each half at two meals, if the napkin was-
n't too soiled. She also lit every match twice, first by striking
the match head, then again later when she touched the
charred matchstick to one stove burner to light another.
Although she bought several loaves of bread a day, Nella
never ate fresh bread. She stashed the new loaves in the refrigerator or breadbox and always ate the day-old bread first.

With a paring knife she cut a cross into the flat bottom of
every new loaf, then wedged it in the crook of her left arm and
hugged it while she carved off thick chunks. I feared for her left
breast. The crust chipped and crackled like the glaze on a raku
pot. In Sicily, after a meal, older women will gather up the
pieces of uneaten bread and kiss them before drying them so
they can be used for breadcrumbs. Nella did not kiss the bread,
but she did put it away to add to tomorrow's breakfast porridge.

Despite receiving several marriage proposals from men
twenty years her senior, Nella had remained single. "Men just
want a slave," she said. Her aunts, uncles, and cousins urged
her to marry for the financial security she'd need when Zia
Carmela died, but Nella didn't want to think about that now.
Maybe someday she'd use her training as a seamstress to take
in tailoring work. For now she was content to be a nurse to her
aunt and a housewife with no husband. She was locally
famous for the clean house she kept, a point of pride among
Sicilian women.

She was not accustomed to leaving the house. The simple
prospect of going for a walk after a meal made Nella nervous,
and a trip to see Carmela's doctor twenty miles away made her

tremble. I have watched her stand at the breadbox for a full hour before departure, in her white suit and heels, tearing chunks off a loaf and eating them anxiously.

"Why do you do this?" I asked.

"Bread gives me strength," she said.

Nella wobbled on her heels. Instead of seeking strength in carbohydrates, I suggested, "Why not wear your comfortable shoes?"

"Comfortable shoes are ugly," she said, and she'd rather be elegant, even if it meant that after fifteen minutes in the street market she'd be leaning heavily on my right arm, trying to get me to bear part of the load. "People judge you by your shoes," Nana had always told me. In Sicily, she was right. Women scanned me from my feet to my face then down to my feet again. Maybe it was the bad sneakers.

Because we were three women alone with no men in the house, other women felt free to visit. Francesca Tuminello was a seventy-year-old widow who lived with her daughter's family across the street. She told me that during the 1940's, shoes were hard to come by in Santa Margherita. "Bandits shot people for the shoes they wore," she said. She knew people who had been robbed of their clothes at gunpoint as they returned from gleaning the grain fields. "They walked home naked, feeling lucky to be alive," she said.

The neighborhood ladies came to visit in the late afternoon, when everyone's morning cleaning chores were done and the men had been fed their dinner and the dishes had been washed and put away. Nella served espresso in polished aluminum demitasse cups. She herself drank no coffee, tea, wine, juice, milk, or soda, nothing but water. Sicilians don't drink from their faucets if they can help it, but prefer water drawn from the springs and fountains of towns that have better water. If someone is going to a good water town, say, Geraci Siculo in the Madonie Mountains, friends will load his car with jugs to be filled at a fountain fed by a mountain stream. Nella drank the water her Uncle Vito drew from the well at his farm in Itria, a mile out of town. She filled a liter bottle from the five-gallon jug she kept under the sink, toweled off the droplets, and poured herself a glass of water.

ॐ   ॐ   ॐ

One morning I found Nella in a panic. She could tell from the gurgling pipes that the town water system was not in service. Fresh tap water had not arrived for eight days now. She feared the tank, which she used for washing, was near empty, and this was putting a crimp in her plans to wash the floors. "Last summer we went twenty days without water," she said.

"Why doesn't the *Giornale di Sicilia* send a reporter to cover this story?" I asked her.

"It's not news," she said. It was a problem all over Sicily. In Santa Margherita one popular explanation for the problem was that the town's water mains were so full of holes that water couldn't make it to the tap. Another was that the pipes were fine but the Mafia-controlled firm that installed them pretended they were in bad shape to qualify for more government money to "fix" them.

Nella had grown up in a stone home, a stronghold. But an earthquake lasting seconds on a cold snowy night in 1968 had crumbled it, forcing her to live in a tent for a year. Then came the humiliation of a metal barrack for nearly twenty years while government reconstruction money got siphoned off in graft before it could reach Santa Margherita. That is why, twenty-four years after the earthquake, many people were still living in temporary barracks. Nella felt lucky to have this home.

While her father still lived and brought in some money, she decorated the house with trinkets, small extravagances: in the sitting room a miniature ceramic clothes iron on a table; above my sofa bed in her late father's room, small framed paintings of a full moon shining over a silvery sea; on the dining-room table the swan-necked vase filled with plastic dahlias; and on the floor in the upstairs hall, the artificial houseplants that caught in Carmela's trailing shawls and were dragged along behind her.

Anything that was "good" in Nella's house was never used. The red ceramic teapot on the back of the stove never felt hot water, the glass cruets on the table never tasted oil or vinegar, and as far as I know I am the only one who has ever sat on the dining-room couch. Nella spread a sheet on it so I did not make contact with the upholstery. This is a genetic condition. When my sister gave my Aunt Freda a new set of pajamas she wouldn't wear them. "They're too good," Aunt Freda said. "Bury me in them." Just like Nana and her daughter, Nella kept the family's priceless handmade lace tablecloths starched stiff in a drawer in the dining room credenza, where they never saw the light of day.

The television was in the dining room, too. At night, Nella and Carmela sat flank to flank in hard wooden chairs and watched *La Ruota della Fortuna,* with the Italian version of Vanna White (younger, more cleavage). Nella crocheted or knitted while she watched. Once every evening she got up to spread a soft blanket over both Carmela's lap and the gas heater on wheels, forming a little heat-tent fire hazard.

No one ever ate at the dining-room table, which took up most of the room and served instead as an altar to deceased family members. Three pictures leaned back in their frames in a semicircle around a votive candle: Nella's father, in his blue cobbler's apron, a broken sandal in his hand, peering over his lunettes, with a widower's button pinned to his crisp, white shirt; Carmela's late husband, looking uncharacteristically serious in a formal black-and-white studio portrait, as though he knew that they might place it under an oval glass on his gravestone and that this sitting must sum up a lifetime; and Zia Betta's drawn face and white hair, a picture taken soon before she died at ninety-three. The faces of the dead stared all day at the flame in the red glass cup.

Every morning the squawk of a roving greengrocer startled me awake. Downstairs I'd find the table set for one: a crisp starched linen towel under my bowl and spoon; the orange plastic sugar bowl set just above the spoon. I found the espresso pot ready to fire up, a liter of milk set beside a clean pot to heat it in, the box of matches in plain sight. It was Monday, washday, and Nella hung the laundry while I drank my bowl of milk and coffee.

Although I was family, Nella treated me like a guest. I was not to cook, clean, or even take care of my own clothes. Besides, if I did, I would be disrupting her routine. She washed my jeans and shirts on a scrub board in a deep sink, reserving the washing machine's scalding temperatures for the sheets. When the week's laundry was dry, she brought it in and ironed it. Ironing was her passion. With a pass of her hand she could flatten mountains, smooth away wrinkles, straighten out a mess.

When the quake struck, Nella was just sixteen, an age when I would have mourned the loss of my Beatles albums or plastic horse collection. I asked Nella what object she lost that she had loved most.

"My iron," she said. I found even my socks and underwear stacked neatly at the foot of my bed, flat as flounder.

When Carmela got up, she sat at the kitchen table and pressed an electric hot water bottle to her belly to warm up. Nella heated some milk in a pan, added a spoonful of tomato sauce, and then cracked an egg into it. The yolk was red because the egg was fresh. The Italian word for yolk is *il rosso*, "the red." She added yesterday's bread, cooked it up and served her aunt. Nella ate her breakfast standing, leaning against the stove for warmth, spooning her porridge straight from the pot. Carmela bent over her bowl, eating in silence, swathed in disheveled layers of black shawls over a plain-cut black dress, worn with black stockings and black shoes, a widow's winter uniform.

Like Nella, Carmela never wanted to marry. But in her middle age, Calogero, a widower, had asked for her hand. He too was a shoemaker, "very sociable," always ready with a joke or some long poem he'd memorized or made up. *"Meroda friotta alla baraoba di chi l'ha scriotta,"* he taught me to say on my first visit. It's nonsense, but if you take out the *o*'s you get, "Fried shit on the beard of him who wrote this." He would crack up whenever I repeated it for him. His pleasures were simple.

At first Carmela turned him down, but then her American cousin Charlie (whom they called "Cholley") convinced her that Calogero was trustworthy, and that if she married him, she wouldn't be alone when her old mother died. Carmela married Calogero when she was almost fifty. They spent their honeymoon in Palermo, a big adventure. The first night they went to a *trattoria*, a small informal eatery, for dinner. "The pasta was raw, truly raw," she whispered, still indignant. And being out on the town unnerved Carmela, who had been raised in a village where a virtuous woman never appeared in public and her name was never heard in the marketplace, the Homerian ideal. So for the rest of the honeymoon, they ordered in, and for the rest of the marriage, Carmela sent her husband to the market with a list. She never went out.

Carmela's brother, then in his seventies, visited daily to check on us women. Vito helped Nella tend her kitchen garden—the grapevines, a clump of mint, artichokes, peas, tomatoes, oregano, fava beans, and prickly pears, this town's chief crop. Here the fruit is called the Indian fig because Columbus brought the plant back from the West Indies. The ovoid fruit comes wrapped in a leathery green casing and looks like a grenade with quills. You have to soak the quills off, then peel the fruit's thick skin with a knife. The flesh, once you reach it, is pink and sweet as sugar cane, shot through with seeds. (Calogero, on a dare, once ate seventy-four prickly pears in a row, and was constipated for days. "It was the seeds," he said.) In the local dialect, the word for the prickly pear is *trummuna*. Out-of-towners call the people of Santa Margherita the *trummunuddu*, the "human prickly pears," but never to their faces.

Once, at lunch, Nella had a tantrum because neither Carmela nor I could eat all that was set before us. Nella pushed her chair back from the table, threw up her arms, and yelled, "I can never do anything right in this house!" She picked up our half-empty bowls of spaghetti and soup and threw them against the kitchen wall. The noodles and sauce dribbled down the tiles. I grabbed my coat and fled out the front door. Carmela never flinched.

"Nella isn't a bad person," Carmela told me later when we were alone. "She's just nervous." Later I learned that Italians have this wonderful custom called *prendere cinque*, "take five," which means that everyone may take five minutes a day to let off steam, and this keeps even cloistered spinsters from going insane.

5

HOME SWEET STONE

❦

THE WAVE OF PROSPERITY that has washed over Sicily in the past thirty years has not reached the summits of the mountains. The earthquake focused the government's attention on the plight of Italy's impoverished south, but the money flowed to the workers in the cities while the populations of the tiny hill towns were pared down to old pensioners. This misfortune had an upside, however. The oldest, highest, most central neighborhoods were saved from renovation or the wrecker's ball. The unchanged town centers stand on the highest peaks besieged by bland cement boxes creeping uphill. Still, you can always walk to the stone heart of a town and block out the twenty-first century.

I have seen houses built of blocks of creamy yellow sandstone, or black lava, or dense blue stones, or pink clay rocks. They grow organically from the bedrock they were built on. Stones are crystals, which vibrate, each at its own frequency. The stones live long, slow lives. A friend of mine has wondered about their consciousness. "Our lives must look like a blur to them," he said. "We probably look like ants running." When I tell my Sicilian friends the houses in Vermont are built of wood, they ask me, aghast, "What happens when the wind blows?"

You can have a friend for years and never see the inside of his house because Sicilians meet each other in piazzas or cafés. The *casa* is sacrosanct, the seraglio where the women stay, so men don't easily bring other men there.

One time a friend invited me to spend an August night in the ultimate stone house—a cave in Sperlinga, an ancient town in the Nebrodi Mountains in the center of Sicily. No one knows when Sperlinga was founded, but people have been living in its cliff caves since the Bronze Age. In the last three decades, most of the townspeople have moved into new cinderblock apartment houses below the cliff, like my friend, Rita, but she had inherited one third of her grandfather's cave home. The cave was in Via Panetteria, a walled ledge carved into the cliff, and had been divided into three sections as the result of an inheritance dispute. The dividing wall was fresh sheet rock. Rita made my bed at the back of the twenty-foot-long tunnel, where it was coolest, and handed me the keys.

My neighbors were the diehards who still lived full-time in their caves. It was a hot summer night and I was company. They pulled their beach chairs out onto the ledge so we could sit and talk. In this odd, absolutely vertical neighborhood cut from the rock face, we watched the moon rise behind the mountains and light the fields below our feet. Living in a cliff has its problems. One young woman complained there was no place for a girl to walk arm in arm with her boyfriend because the cliff paths were too narrow. One lady said she wanted to add a room but was not allowed because the Sperlinga caves are listed on the Italian equivalent of the National Historic Register and she was not allowed to dig farther into the cliff. But one man said that when the 1968 earthquake shook all of Sicily, he moved back into his cave home, which was safer. "The mountain won't fall around your ears," he said. At midnight they folded their chairs and we all slept inside the mountain.

Next morning I was dressed and out early. Signora Placenti of the cave next door was scrubbing the ledge in front of her house with a broom and soapy water. Sicilian women clean their homes furiously in the mornings. On ladders, they attack walls, windows, and ceiling lamps. Every day, sometimes twice, they dust, mop floors and stairs, wipe down the walls, degrease the stove, and polish their expensive wooden front doors. They shake mops from their balconies, snap rags out of windows, and disappear again quickly as the fluff floats down slowly onto the laundry on other people's lines. They clean with such gusto that I wonder whether they are thinking of the years when they had nothing to dust.

Signora Placenti, my cave neighbor, was a short red-haired woman in her sixties. She invited me in for coffee and a look at her rare two-story cave.

It was dark inside, normal for a house whose only windows are holes punched in the rock. She turned on a light. Except for the tile floor, she had covered every inch of rock surface with wainscoting, including the walls, the ceiling, the stairwell, and the steps. She had a microwave, a gas stove, a television, a videotape player, running water, and a full-sized tub in the bathroom. The dining-room credenza displayed her wedding crystal. A clear plastic sheet covered a cutwork cloth on the table. She made espresso and we gabbed in the kitchen. "My husband is a farmer," she told me. Their daughter and grandchild lived in the cave next door. Then she took me upstairs to see her pride and joy.

Her bedroom was also covered with thin strips of wood, but she had left her son's room au naturel, the only rock wall left exposed in the house. He slept in this cubbyhole room, all curved and womblike, when he vacationed from his factory job in Torino. Its bumpy walls were stippled with light from the French doors Mrs. Placenti now opened with a flourish. They gave onto the balcony, a lip of rock jutting from the cliff face. Red geraniums bloomed in pots at our feet. We stepped back inside and looked through the stone portal at the deep, bright valley of golden-brown wheat stalks.

"See that door?" she asked.

"Yes."

"It used to be a window. But it was always so dark in here. One day, I sent my husband off to work, found his sledgehammer, and I made the window into a door."

She folded her arms across her breast and vibrated fiercely. "Our Lord was born in a cave, and we live in one."

6

SATURDAY MARKET

꒰ꩰ꒱

NELLA BOUGHT HER TRINKETS—the plastic plants, the ceramic iron, the silver seascapes on the wall—at the Saturday street market. Every country village has a market day when out-of-town vendors in mobile vans take over a main street, undercut the local merchants, make a mess, and leave before lunch. For Nella, market day was the social event of the week.

She got up extra early, went into the ground-floor bathroom (only I, the guest, was to use the "good" pink-tiled bathroom upstairs, with matching pink tub and bidet), and took a sponge bath standing at the sink. Water was scarce and expensive to heat. She changed from her at-home skirt into something constricting, then called our friends, the Abruzzo sisters, Rosetta and Giuseppina, to see if they'd pick us up in their old Fiat 500. Rosetta was in her forties, tall and big-boned, with a smooth white complexion, perfect teeth, high cheekbones, and a beatific smile. She had never married, and had no children and no worry lines. She made me think of a nun in civvies. The sisters' parents and three of their brothers had died, but Rosetta still cooked and cleaned for a middle-aged brother in whose house the sisters lived. Her smile hid a life of sacrifice. She was the one who knew how to drive.

Her older sister, Giuseppina, was short and squat, and her head sank down between her shoulders, like an owl's. She suffered from arthritis so she wrapped herself in two black shawls, which was easier than getting into a coat. Once I gave her all my American aspirin because she believed they were more powerful than her own. She did not speak Italian; I rarely understood her without a translation by her sister. Giuseppina had never married either. If they'd give us a ride, Nella could stand the pain of her shoes long enough to buy staples for the week. We'd be four spinsters on a spree.

The sisters picked us up. First stop was the chapel in a cave near the entrance to Santa Margherita, the only church that hadn't crumbled in the earthquake. The sisters owned the cave, which was on land they'd inherited. Brides stopped here after their weddings to leave their bouquets for good luck. Giuseppina and Rosetta ironed the priest's brocade chasubles, laundered his white albs, collected the change from the offering box, stocked the banks of flickering red votive candles, and changed the flowers in the vases on the altar steps. Giuseppina was also the custodian of the miraculous image of the Virgin that had cured a deaf man by ordering him to pour oil in his ear. Blind in one eye, Giuseppina squinted and fixed me with the other. "Worms crawled out!" she said.

Word spread and people made pilgrimages to ask for miracles. The hammered silver ex-votos they offered in exchange hung in a glass case near the altar. They were the symbolic ears, breasts, kidneys, lungs, legs, and eyes of sick people who had prayed to this image of the Virgin and had been cured. Cards attached to each miniature silver body part read: "For Grace Received." The bas-relief trinkets were costly sacrifices for the plain people who left them here. Among the body parts stood silver silhouettes of well-dressed gentlemen. "Some women prayed for a husband," Giuseppina explained.

The ex-votos offered by the poorest were instead wax models shaped and colored by a craftsman. These life-sized three-dimensional body parts hung ghoulishly from ropes tied to the dark rafters in the back of the church. Above me a pair of yellow breasts sagged earthward, a tumor on the right dripping blood like a poked yolk. The wax feet, hands, heads, and organs were strangely elongated and coated with soot. A penis and an infant drooped among them, Dali-esque. "There was a fire and they melted," Giuseppina said. She was cleaning the banks of votive candles, clinking them rhythmically. When they finished their church work we drove to the market.

Since her father's death Nella only looked at plastic flowers and bought groceries instead: pounds of pasta, a string bag of oranges with the leaves still on their stems, a chunk of parmesan wrapped in waxy white paper, an armful of lettuce and spinach with the dirt still clinging to the roots. Then she went to the butcher's van to buy meat that wasn't neither quite veal nor beef, but it was bovine. (It costs too much to raise a calf to steak-hood.) Mottled sausages cascaded from hooks like a curtain between client and butcher. A skinned lamb hung by its delicate hind hooves, bound together by a cord, its belly split open from genitals to throat. A stick spread its ribs to show its fresh, pink innards. All the while I kept my eye on two fearsome yellow dogs with no collars looking for bloody bones thrown out behind the butcher's van.

The Abruzzo sisters, middle-aged maidens in mourning, wandered over to the tent where a vendor sold black dresses, black stockings, black slippers, black shoes, black bras, black slips, black kerchiefs, black umbrellas, black shawls, black purses, black sweaters, and black coats—one-stop shopping for the female bereaved. Men in mourning wear only a black cloth-covered button pinned to the shirt or lapel, and even that is optional. Many older widows remain married to their dead husbands, and wear gold chains with a locket containing a copy of the photo that is also on his gravestone. Second marriages are frowned upon among women of a certain age. "Love is for life," they say, and if you take a second husband, the sincerity of your intentions in your first marriage may be questioned. But widowers may take a second wife (she is called the bride "of the second bed") because the men may have children to raise and need a helpmate.

I was Nella's mule that day—she bought, I carried. Milling all around us were stunning teenage girls—olive-skinned beauties with flawless faces, thick flowing hair, flat bellies, and Sophia Loren attitude—dutifully being mules for their mothers, the thick-waisted, hairy-moled matrons they might one day become. *How does it happen? And when?* I pondered this, and felt my face for signs of moles.

I looked at the comfortable clothes. It was hard to find a sweatshirt without something written on it in English. The script didn't have to make sense to sell the shirt. One had so much writing that I took notes. It said, all over it:

Rocks of the Field
West Story
Designed by Chief Long Lance
For the American Boys
Who Enjoy Indian
Enjoy an exclusive
Line a Indian Conception
Western One

Go figure.

Down the Via San Francesco, past the food booths, the outdoor market turned into a world-beat Woolworth's. The day was cold and cloudy. Two very black Africans stood mute and as still as statues behind the row of hanging black leather belts they had hand-tooled. No one was buying. A Sicilian craftsman sold brass sheep bells for about four dollars apiece. A miserable wet wind blew down the street. A young Arab merchant brooded over his tray of mirrored sunglasses. He saw me eyeing his display from afar and smelled a sale.

He waved me over and handed me his fifty-dollar top-of-the-line sunglasses to try on.

"I don't have that kind of money," I said. He thought I was bargaining and stepped up his sales pitch. I asked for a mirror and he handed me one—a rearview car mirror, still in its bubble pack, borrowed from the car parts dealer next to him.

I had promised myself a pair of sunglasses one afternoon when I was out walking and met the mattress man on his monthly rounds from nearby Castelvetrano. He cruised the streets of mountain towns in a flatbed truck loaded with singles and *matrimoniali* in precarious stacks and hawked them through a loudspeaker on the cab roof. His voice sounded oddly stretched, so that when he passed I looked at his face to see whether his lips were moving or that was a worn-out tape he was playing. A look is a powerful thing in Sicily, where people believe in the Evil Eye and love is declared with a furtive glance in church. A misplaced look can bring trouble. Shades are eye curtains that shield you from the prying, measuring, or leering looks of others. The trouble was that the mattress man had seen me focusing on his lips when a virtuous woman wouldn't even have looked up. He coasted just behind me, staring a hole in the back of my head. When I turned in at Nella's house he hit the brakes hard and his mattresses slithered down all over one another. Nella opened the door for me and looked over my shoulder at this stranger in the truck eating me with his eyes. She pulled me in, closed the door quickly, and went to peek from behind a lacy curtain while I changed into my sweats.

When I came back downstairs, Nella was still at the window. "Take a look! He's waiting for you!" The driver stared at our door but he didn't get out of the truck, not even to re-stack his mattresses, and when I looked again in five minutes, he was gone. *Next time I go out*, I promised myself, *I'll wear shades*.

7

WASH ON THE LINE

སྗᘘ

"WELL HUNG, HALF IRONED." That's what the women say about hanging wet laundry. It's a folk art—the draping without wrinkles, the juxtapositions of shapes and colors, the shock of white sheets. The wash line tells a story in a semaphore code anyone can read. Without speaking or even being seen, a woman can say: "Ha! I have my wash hung before you're even up." Or she can hang boys' briefs, men's work clothes, and black shawls to say: "I have three sons, two are out of diapers, my husband's got a job, and my widowed mother lives with us." You can tell from her wet laundry if a woman is lonely or overworked, or how many times she will patch her husband's pants before letting him wear the new ones. And a woman can signal her lover it is safe to come up by leaving only her nightgown on the line.

I have only seen a dryer once in Sicily, and that was in my American girlfriend's house. Appliances and the fuel to run them are expensive. And in Sicily the sun shines most of the time anyway. Pinning laundry to a line is an excuse for a woman to be outside, or at least to linger on her balcony without being deemed wanton.

I have seen, in Giuliana, laundry flutter like prayer flags from a line strung between a balcony and a church steeple. I have seen sheets strung across a cobblestone street in Locati where they would have blocked traffic had there been any. The woman who hung them had washed them in a tin tub, sloshed the rinse water onto the stones, and swept the stones while they were wet. The whites were wrung into tight gourds ready to be snapped flat and pinned up. The white-haired woman hid behind a sheet when she saw me, a stranger with a camera. When I asked to take her picture, she stepped in front of the sheets taken from the bed she still shares with her husband and smiled sweetly.

I had heard that in Geraci Siculo there lived an American woman who had married a man from Palermo. They had met in London, where they both had jobs. Neither she nor her husband had family in this town in the Madonie Mountains but had moved there with their two young daughters, from England and out of the blue, because the town was beautiful—a very un-Sicilian thing to do. One day I found her. Melissa Gay Rose was a former dancer and contortionist from Mississippi. Her clothesline was closely watched.

She had made concessions to the culture when she moved here. "I don't iron underwear, towels, or sheets, but I do iron everything else," she said. One day she hung five identical black socks on her line. A week passed, another washday, and she hung another five socks. That afternoon a neighbor lady she rarely spoke to hailed her in the street and said, "Oh, Rosa, I am so glad you found your husband's other sock. I said a prayer that you would find it."

8

THE SHEEP SLEEP IN PALACES

ॐ

ONE MORNING IN LATE WINTER, when life begins again in the Sicilian countryside, Nella's uncle, Vito, brought me to the cliff at the highest and oldest part of Santa Margherita to look down on the green and brown hills, billowing like a sheet settling over a giant, voluptuous woman. Slow clouds trailed their shadows over her curves. Magpies cavorted in a stiff wind and walking rain fell on the grapevines. Vito pointed down at an outcropping of stones. "There's an Arab cemetery down there," he said. "Skulls used to pop out of the ground and we would use them for soccer balls." On the crests of hills below us stood other, venerable towns all shaken by the earthquake: Sambuca di Sicilia, Poggioreale, Salaparuta, and, far off to the left, Gibellina, the quake's epicenter.

The old Santa Margherita had been abandoned and the palace that had been its soul lay in pieces on the ground. Unlatched shutters banged in the wind, the sun shone through cracks into rooms never meant to see the light. I took a picture of an arched stone doorway, made of golden limestone blocks, the keystone missing, the arch still standing. Cruel purple thistles with dark-green leaves covered the old deserted piazza, a no man's land where shepherds penned their flocks and tarry black sheep dung coated the streets. Every morning they milked their ragged long-tailed ewes in nobles' courtyards and kitchens.

Every evening at around four, the shepherds brought their flocks up out of the fields. The sheep drank from the mossy watering trough before a shepherd herded them into the Scaminaci Palace courtyard and shut the door for the night milking. The mountain shepherds were a wild breed themselves, sometimes hired as hit men because they knew the country hideouts. One threw stones at me to make me move out of his flock's way. When I described him to Nella she told me his wife had just disappeared one day; locals suspected he had killed her and burned her body in a bread oven, but the police never investigated, she said.

During the day, when the shepherd was gone, I roamed these old ruins. The sandstone walls were warm and rough as dry sponges; I could pick thick pieces of seashell out of them. The houses were cubes and rectangles. I climbed up crumbling staircases and found sheep droppings in the salons, dining rooms, boudoirs, and bedrooms. I thought to myself, "This is the real last chapter to *The Leopard*," a great novel of the decline of the Sicilian aristocracy. "The sheep sleep in broken palaces."

The most important house in town was the Palazzo Cutò-Filangeri, where *The Leopard*'s author, Giuseppe di

Lampedusa, born in 1896 of noble blood, actually spent his boyhood summers. "Set in the middle of town, right on the leafy square," he wrote in his memoirs, "it spread over a vast expanse and contained about a hundred rooms, large and small. It gave the impression of an enclosed and self-sufficient entity, of a kind of Vatican as it were, that included state rooms, living rooms, quarters for thirty guests, servants' rooms, three enormous courtyards, a large and very lovely garden, and a great orchard."

Six years after his memoirs were published, the earthquake left only the palace's façade standing. It sliced the church in half lengthwise, splitting it open so that every afternoon the sun's last rays nestled into the concave curve of its lapis-blue domed ceiling. Still intact was the bamboo screen in front of the balcony seats so that a princess might attend Mass without being stared at.

The palace was the pride of the town. In *The Leopard,* di Lampedusa sent the lovers, Tancredi and Angelica, wandering through its labyrinth of rooms. Vito's wife, Grazia, once told me the palace had "so many rooms it took an hour and a half to open all the windows, and an hour and a half to close them." Portraits of di Lampedusa's ancestors, dating back to 1080, once lined the entrance hall in a double row. In the second half of the twentieth century, the palace was sold. Antonio Giambalvo, a carpenter then in his sixties, told me that when he was thirteen years old the new owners hired him to salvage what could be sold. Because he was light they sent him up the scaffolding with a knife to cut painted panels off the ceiling. "They sold the paintings for I don't know how much, but they gave us twenty thousand lire for each one we sliced off the ceiling," he said. He found antique guns behind some paintings.

The palace was old but the town was much older. The palace had been built around the remains of an Arab lookout tower. People had been living in Santa Margherita since the Bronze Age. Nomadic Berbers and other Arabs from what is now Tunisia settled this town in 826 and named it Manzil Sindi, a name it kept for centuries, Italianized as Misilsindo. Manzil Sindi was a stronghold that, at 1,500 feet above sea level, was the highest hill in the region. North African Arabs ruled Sicily from 827 to 1060, bringing with them citrus trees, olives, palms, durum wheat, dome-topped mosques, poets, geographers, subterranean irrigation canals, fountains, harems, hidden courtyards, intellectuals who translated the Greek classics into Arabic, and excellent fiscal administration. Invading Normans took the last Arab stronghold in 1060, but they kept the Arabs on to run things in what is now considered Sicily's Golden Age. In the late fourteenth century the settlement became the feudal estate of Baron Antonio Corbera, a Spanish nobleman. The local wine still bears his name. In the 1600's the Corberas built the palaces that endured until the 1968 earthquake, and renamed the town to honor the patron saint of Margherita Resquesens, the baron's mother.

"She was beautiful," the old ladies say of this town, always with a circular wave of the hand to indicate delight. Every stone tells a story. Vito and I were standing in San Vito, the ninth-century neighborhood where he was born, at the base of what used to be a minaret where a muezzin once called the faithful to prayer. It doubled as a lookout tower. In the seventeenth century the minaret became the steeple of the Church of San Calojero and the people nicknamed it Babbaluce, "the snail," because an external staircase spiraled up it as a snail would climb a pole. Now the minaret is in a pile on the ground—a jumble of stones, weeds, and broken majolica tiles, white, blue, and yellow. In its place rises a steel transmission tower for Silvio Berlusconi's television network.

One evening Vito introduced me to Professor Salvatore Scuderi, a historian who for the past twenty years had been writing the town's history. He showed me his four-inch-thick manuscript, for which he already had a publisher, but he was blocked at January 15, 1968. I didn't need to ask why; he was in love with the proud, elegant town that died that day.

The professor used to edit and write *L'Araldo (The Herald)*, a town periodical that announced births, deaths, and marriages, along with local news and historical features. In the town's library, then housed in a Quonset hut, I found back issues describing glittering evenings of dance in the Leopard's garden, now the town park, where the moon reflected in the tiered pools of a fountain that the prince once kept stocked with Belice River eels for his table. Prince Alessandro II Filangeri, di Lampedusa's ancestor, planted the park's oldest trees in the middle of the eighteenth century. Queen Maria Carolina of the Bourbon court walked among the palms, bamboo, and orange trees when, a fugitive, she spent three months here in 1812 and 1813 as the guest of another of Lampedusa's forebears.

In the 1960's *L'Araldo* recorded the election of beauty queens—Miss Bellezza, Miss Eleganza, Miss Simpatia. Santa Margherita itself was so beautiful that it was often the setting for films, like Germi's *Seduced and Abandoned* and Visconti's *The Leopard,* both released in 1963. The ball scene was filmed in the Palazzo Cutò-Filangeri. Burt Lancaster played Prince Corbera and Claudia Cardinale played Angelica, his nephew's fiancée. Some of my relatives had bit parts but flubbed them. Calogero, Carmela's late husband, played a dead soldier but was cut from the film because he swatted at flies drawn to the cherry-preserve blood smeared on his face. After the earthquake, the town was the setting for one more film, *Anno Zero,* about the world on the day after an atomic war.

9

THE EARTHQUAKE

କ୍ଷୁ

WHEN I MET MARGHERITA CACIOPPO in the winter of 1992, she was a bright, vivacious, thirty-four-year-old architect with curly black hair and a warm smile that made us friends right away. She was nine years old when the earthquake struck. We sat in her mansard apartment while she told me what she remembered.

The fourteenth of January, 1968, was a Sunday, and Margherita was home with her mother. Her family had lived in their house for generations. The electrician was there, fixing something in the kitchen. Just before noon they felt the wall tremble and heard the windows rattle, and Margherita, instinctively, without ever having felt an earthquake or even heard of one, said to her mother, "Mom! It's an earthquake!" Her mother slapped her so hard she split Margherita's lip. "Be quiet!" her mother yelled. "You shouldn't say such things. God will punish you." Margherita cried. In the space of a few minutes, the street filled with people, and children were out on their balconies crying.

The town had no recorded history of seismic activity; the tower of the Church of San Calojero, built 1,100 years before as a minaret, still stood without a crack in it until that afternoon. A neighbor, Signora Giovanna, yelled to Margherita's mother from her balcony across the street: "Mica! Mica! What was that?"

Her mother spread her arms apart. Nobody had the courage to say that word, earthquake. Signora Giovanna's husband yelled to her, "Get in here right now." Then everything calmed down and they switched on the radio and heard there had been a tremor in the Belice River valley. The epicenter was at Gibellina, but several other towns had been shaken—Santa Ninfa, Montevago, Salaparuta, and Poggioreale. Then they didn't think much more about it.

The town was quiet for a few hours. At five in the afternoon, Margherita went to Mass with her mother at the Church of San Francesco, built in the 1700's. She was wearing a new dress and the new patent leather shoes her mother had bought her for Christmas, and she walked between her relatives, who held her hands and lifted her over the slush piles in the streets. It had snowed the night before, which was strange for this town.

In church, the Mass progressed to the Consecration. Padre Scaturro raised the host with both arms over his head. This was the Transubstantiation, the moment when the bread would become the body of Christ. The ground shook as the altar boy rang the altar bells. "I saw the floor tiles rise up in a ripple," Margherita said. "They were ceramic tiles, hand-painted in many colors." Padre Scaturro put down the still unconsecrated host. "Don't worry," he said, "because we are in the house of God." But he finished Mass in a hurry. People put their hands to their heads and walked home. Margherita and her mother walked to her uncle's house, where they saw a news bulletin on his black-and-white television. The belltower of a church in Gibellina had fallen. From their own mother church next to the Leopard's palace, only some of the outside trim had come off. They wondered whether the tremors were local or all of Italy had been affected.

"That night after supper, we went home, still very upset. My father was in Switzerland, working. My oldest brother was at university in Palermo. That meant my twelve-year-old brother, Andrea, was the head of the family." Usually Andrea stayed out late on Sundays, even though he was only twelve, but that night he came home early.

One of Margherita's aunts walked down from San Vito. She said it wouldn't be right for all of them to go home and go to bed as usual. And her mother said they shouldn't separate. "At least we should all die together," Margherita's mother said. They stayed together until twelve-thirty that night, then split up, thinking nothing more would happen after the initial two tremors.

After a while they went to bed. Her brother was scared, so they both snuggled up in their mother's big bed. Directly overhead was another aunt's sitting room. They heard their Aunt Anna and Uncle Pasquale walking around upstairs so they didn't feel so alone. Her brother had to pee, but he wanted Margherita to come with him. She walked him to the bathroom, then they went back to bed. After twenty minutes they fell asleep.

"Then we heard it, the end of the world." A booming rumble, a deep, hollow sound, like thunder, like an avalanche, it lasted fifteen seconds. The town rolled on waves of earth. The ground split and swallowed buildings. All ten churches in town crashed to the ground. In the time it took for Margherita and Andrea to wake up and clutch each other, the streets below filled with shouting men and wailing women. The crowd was terrified.

Her uncle from upstairs was banging on the door. "Mica! Mica! Get out!" Margherita's mother told him they were in their pajamas. "Open or I'll bust this door down." Her mother opened for Uncle Pasquale. He told them to get dressed. Margherita put on her new dress, the one she'd worn to church. She asked her mother which shoes she should wear—her old shoes or the patent-leather ones? Her mother started to cry. "Don't worry. Don't worry," she said over and over. Her brother cried, too. He got dressed, went outside, and took his sister with him. Their mother wouldn't budge. "No, I'm staying here," she said.

The tremors were coming one right after another, ten minutes apart. Her aunt and uncle grabbed her mother by her arms and pulled her out of the bedroom by force. In that instant, the floor of her aunt's sitting room fell onto her mother's bed. It left a hole in the ceiling four feet wide, exactly the shape of the bed.

"In the street, pandemonium. The electricity was out, the lights were gone. The snow, the people were slipping and falling in the snow." With every tremor, another building crumbled and fell to the ground, and a cloud of dust and pulverized sandstone rose up from where a home had stood for centuries. Babies were crying. "We thought it was the end. We all expected to die, right there in the middle of our street," Margherita said. "It was chaos." When her mother came out, there was another violent tremor. Her aunt and her mother picked up a black shawl. They "called all of us together—cousins, brothers, aunts, uncles, all the relatives—and draped it over our heads, so we all could die together." They didn't want their children to see what was happening, their houses collapsing in a roar.

"Then, silence. The houses weren't falling anymore." The streets were full of cars now, their headlights on. Margherita's uncle ran to tell her grandparents that they were still alive. Her aunt ran back upstairs to get the family's cash and gold jewelry. Just then there was the strongest tremor of all, and the outer staircase fell apart. Her aunt couldn't get back down to the street, so her daughter ripped a door off its hinges and laid it over the rubble so her mother could slide down. She remembered with her child's eye: "My aunt was fat; she came down with her legs apart. You could see her underpants." Her uncle fetched his car. "Get in," he said to Margherita's grandparents. "You take the children," her grandfather said. "I'm staying here. Even if I die, I am ninety years old and it doesn't matter. You all go."

Everyone was headed for the countryside, where many had orchards and some livestock. The boys collected wood and made a fire. It was January 15. It was freezing. She listened to what the grown-ups were saying. The end of the world had come. She heard her mother say, "I'll never go home again."

They heard screams coming from Montevago; it was very near. "We saw the dust rise from Montevago." They were in the open country, and every time there was a tremor, Margherita saw a deep trench open in the dark, then seal up again. The ground kept opening and closing, a hungry mouth. There would be a rumble like thunder, then dogs would bark, then came a tremor, and her eyes always went to the ground. Deeper into the night, Margherita heard the drone of helicopters and the roaring of the earth. All night, until the next morning, it rained. The boys and her uncle cut the branches off a fruit tree and made a lean-to. "Other families came to us. The old people stayed in the cars." Her uncle went back to town to look for her grandfather. They found him at the bridge at the edge of town, quietly drinking wine. "All this happened because man is evil," he said. "This is the apocalypse. It is God's punishment for our sins."

At the same time, Margherita's aunts had commandeered her grandfather's country cottage and had broken in to get at the dishes, the knives and forks, and the olive oil and salt. It was now six in the morning; to eat something hot, they cooked pasta. They drew water from the well, and her uncle took money and went back to town. He was able to buy four kilos of spaghetti, but the store owner made him pay double.

Her aunts cooked for thirty people, but there weren't enough plates for everybody.

" 'Don't worry, I'll get plates for you,' my grandfather said, and he went off and cut the leaves from the prickly pear plants." The slightly concave succulent leaves form shallow bowls. "My grandfather soaked the leaves in well water, removed all the quills, and I ate my spaghetti from a *figo d'india* leaf, with a spoon." In the meantime, Gibellina and Montevago had been leveled. Every house was gone. "At Santa Margherita thirty lay dead," Margherita said. "At Montevago, one hundred twenty. In Gibellina, more than two hundred. We fell asleep."

The dead who could be found were taken to a temporary morgue at the elementary school. In a few days, one of Margherita's uncles traveled the fifty miles from Palermo over a road that hardly existed anymore to pick them up in a van. It took two trips to remove all his relatives to safety. Earthquake victims began a diaspora that took them to Sciacca, then Palermo, then Agrigento, on the southwest coast. It was three days before Margherita could bathe and change out of her Christmas dress.

"When my father saw the news on Swiss television, he cried, he told us later. In the meantime, the head of our family was my twelve-year-old brother." At the refugee camp they brought him pants that were so big he had to hold them up with one hand until the chief of police came along and gave him his own belt. Meanwhile, back in Santa Margherita, the government had set up a tent city. Resident survivors had barricaded the entrance to town. "The people there hated us because we left. 'We stayed here to suffer and you went away,' they told us when we returned to salvage some furniture.

"We stayed in Agrigento for a year, then they said we could go home because they had built us barracks. And we returned to Santa Margherita, to the metal and plywood barracks, ice cold in winter, witheringly hot in summer."

Margherita grew up in those "temporary" barracks, twenty years of living in humiliating conditions, with bedspreads hung from clotheslines for interior walls, while federal money for rebuilding the town was siphoned off to contractors and politicians in bribes and kickbacks. By the late eighties, when the town was finally rebuilt, most of its houses were opulent boxes with plumbing, designed by "foreigners" from northern Italy.

That is why Margherita grew up to become an architect. I've seen some of the houses she designed. They show verve and character. One has a hanging garden built into a scalloped outer baluster; a few have mansard apartments like her own. The most striking feature of Margherita's own home, which she shares with her mother, is an outrageous seven-foot-high, ten-foot-wide freestanding arch that bends over the third-floor balcony like a stone rainbow. I asked her if it was an allusion to the sign God sent Noah after the deluge—a symbol of his promise never again to destroy the world by flood. I thought she was saying: No More Earthquakes.

I could think what I wanted, Margherita said. "It's art."

For her the arch evokes a spirit from another world, the fabric of another life. She placed it over the highest balcony to remind her and those who pass below it of all the arched, recessed doorways, the vaulted ceilings, the curve of the dome-topped mosque, the twisting alleys, all the soft, rounded shapes, the well-loved contours of the Santa Margherita she knew until she was nine.

10

POLIZZI GENEROSA

ॐ

ONE SPRING I RENTED AN APARTMENT on the edge of a cliff in the Madonie Mountains in north-central Sicily, forty minutes south of Cefalù, on the northern coast. My kitchen balcony hung out over a valley so deep it made me dizzy. I looked down on the backs of soaring magpies. The earth dropped away in tiers; my knees went weak at the view. On tiny natural terraces on the V-shaped walls of the canyon, celery-green pastures clung to the outcroppings like rags blown about by the wind.

The woman who lived below me kept a kitchen garden below my balcony. When the wind blew my laundry off my balcony clothesline, my panties would snag on her artichokes, an embarrassing situation. Below her garden, the road made its last hairpin curve into town. Every night at blue dusk a man rode a mule sidesaddle up out of the fields below. He dropped the reins to button his collar against the March wind. The mule carried home his own supper and tomorrow's breakfast, two giant golden balls of hay in rope sacks, one at each hip. The mule and I were neighbors in Via Collesano, three thousand feet above sea level.

I found Polizzi one day when I was staring at my old map. I would point to the tiny towns and say their honey-flow names aloud to myself. *Raffadali, Linguaglossa, Acquaviva, Collesano, Racalmuto, Mussomeli, Cefalù.* I spiraled my finger around the middle of Sicily. *Polizzi Generosa*, a long name for a small dot. Was there some story here about generous policemen? I planned to take a bus there, but then I met Joseph.

One afternoon in Santa Margherita, visitors filled Nella's sitting room. Three gray-haired neighbor ladies huddled with Carmela on folding chairs around the portable gas heater. Maria Elisa, her husband, and I drew three more chairs into the circle. Every time a new batch of people arrived, Nella brewed more espresso. Everyone was talking very fast. Someone knocked, then a young man with a cap of curly black hair let himself in. It was Joseph—I was told he was a distant cousin—come to meet me.

He stood stiffly at the door, his knees locked under him, nervously adjusting his glasses, which had fogged. They were black-rimmed with thick lenses. He wore a plaid wool jacket and jeans. He looked smart, a little nerdy. His hair was short and nappy. More furry black hair covered the backs of his hands, curled over the top of his pressed white shirt, and sprouted in wiry bunches from both ears. "But my eyebrows don't meet in the middle," he pointed out to me. "That is my saving grace."

He was thirty-one, young enough to be considered a boy in Sicily. Joseph seemed considerate, respectful of his elders, and flattering. When he worked a room, the women felt prettier, the men more clever. "It doesn't cost anything to be nice," he always said. Old ladies loved him. The ones in this room scooted over to let him wedge into the circle. He sat down on a spaghetti-webbed chair opposite me and looked me right in the eye.

"Why are you here?" he asked.

"Because my grandparents were born here, and because I love Sicily. I'm writing about what life is like here." He seemed satisfied, and in the next few months, he never asked me another question about myself.

We talked back and forth above four white heads. The ink was still wet on his engineering degree but people now called him *Dottore*. He was the only freelance construction engineer in a town that had just received $140 million from the federal government to finish up post-earthquake construction. (Miracles do happen in election years.) His name really was Joseph, not Giuseppe, because he was born in northern France, where his father had emigrated to find work. When he was born, the doctor who delivered him asked his mother the child's name. "She said 'Giuseppe,' but the doctor wrote 'Joseph,' the French translation, on my birth certificate," he explained.

Commissions were scarce at the start of his career, but Sicilians are skilled at cobbling together a living. Joseph was the local correspondent for the island's two dailies and managed a radio station and a local weekly paper in nearby Menfi. He was a founder of Barak-esh, a grassroots association of thirty-somethings who grew up in Santa Margherita's barracks town and fought to get the people into permanent homes. And at the moment, he had a substitute-teaching job at a high school in Polizzi Generosa.

"Come with me to Palermo tomorrow night," he said. "The next morning we'll drive to Polizzi."

The next night, Joseph and I drove in silence past the dark, empty shells of the shattered old town on the crest of the hill in Santa Margherita. As we coasted down the other side, I saw two glittering pools of light puddling up on the hillsides across the Belice River valley. They were the blue-white streetlights of the new towns of Salaparuta and Poggioreale. The old villages, their hilltop predecessors, had gone dark in the earthquake. Unlike in the States, where cities trail off into suburbs, Sicilian hill towns have clearly defined borders. Here the village is for living in and the land is for crops. When we descended into the valley, Salaparuta set behind the rounded hills, and a giant melon-rind moon, the color of blood, rose and hovered above us.

It was fifty miles to Palermo, where we'd spend the night in a student-rented apartment owned by Joseph's brother, who had moved to Scotland to teach Italian to the emigrants' children. From the Palermo apartment we'd take off early the next morning, pick up another substitute teacher, and drive east to Cefalù, then head south to lofty Polizzi Generosa, a total of seventy miles. As we neared Palermo that evening, we saw the city lit up, dazzling, jutting into the black sea. Fireworks rocketed up from some *quartiere* feasting a saint. They burst in air then glittered down in silent, surreal arcs.

"Palermo by night," Joseph said, in postcard English, as if he were laying the city at my feet.

I spent the night in a room plastered with peace posters. The students who lived there shifted around to accommodate me. The next morning at seven, Joseph and I were at the substitute teachers' bar to pick up our rider. Bars serve more pastries and espresso than liquor, but you can always have your coffee "corrected" with brandy, or whatever you choose. Every bar has its own personality and specialty clientele. This was the substitute teachers' bar. Here they met their carpool rides to go to their far-flung mountain-town assignments. The place was always packed because full-time teachers took advantage of the liberal leave policies available to them, and unemployed professionals signed up in droves to take their places. A half dozen subs were headed to Polizzi alone, but Joseph's only rider was Giuseppina, a gym teacher.

We took the Circonvallazione, a dangerous, garbage-strewn highway that rings the city, and passed a man driving sixty miles an hour with his nose buried in a newspaper. I wondered if he was reading the front-page story about how dangerous the Circonvallazione was: an accident every nineteen hours, a death every thirty days. Gasoline cost about five dollars a gallon then. Joseph drove eight hundred miles a week and spent half his paycheck on gas, which, like wine, is sold by the liter.

The last half hour of the trip to Polizzi was straight up. At every hairpin curve, Joseph's briefcase slid and thumped in the trunk. I sat in the backseat, turning green. We ascended past olive groves, hazelnut trees, and almond and pear orchards in bloom. We saw the deep-wrinkled necks of older farmers in straw hats who hacked at the soil between trees. March is the season for cultivation in the mountains of Sicily, before the sun gets too hot in April. I stuck my head out the window and sniffed the air. Up here it was chilled champagne. The higher we climbed, the stronger was my sensation that we were leaving the physical world behind and entering a more ethereal one.

A spring snow powdered the highest mountaintops across the broad greening valley. Blossoming fruit trees fizzed pink and white. Below us shaving-cream clouds floated into the valley and hovered, casting blue shadows on the earth. When a cloud crashed slowly into a mountain, it slithered wormlike over the peak and down the other side. The last hairpin curve brought us under a hundred-foot cliff topped by a row of two-story apartments that came flush with the cliff edge, their balconies leaning dizzily over the abyss.

Joseph parked the car and the three of us went to a railing outside the Bellavista Bar to take in the beautiful view. A cloud collided with our mountain and we were lost in a luminous mist. Eyes wide open I could see only the white light inside a cloud. I floated bodiless, untethered, in a white splendor. The door to some heaven was opened; this was my welcome to Polizzi.

No one spoke as the veil slowly lifted and we drifted half-dazed into the dark bar. Such moments of rapture happen more often in Sicily than anywhere else I've been.

The bar was unmanned. The owner was in the backroom playing cards. A cardboard sign taped to the top shelf of liquor bottles begged us not to smoke. The hand-lettered sign bore *francobolli,* the stamps that every sign must display. Baby-sitters, English tutors, people with rooms to rent, all must pay a tax to display their printed flyers. To avoid this tax on advertising, some businesses hang their store signs upside down. We drank our coffee, then the teachers went to work and I took a walk.

ॐ ॐ ॐ

The streets of Polizzi are narrow and nubby with cobblestones the color of old nickels. Walking is easy because horizontal streets terrace the town. Some of the vertical connecting lanes are stone staircases, some are thousand-year-old Arab tunnels. The Corso Garibaldi, Polizzi's level main street, bisects the town into upper and lower. Its straight half-mile starts at the stone-paved Piazza Gramsci, where older men soak up the sun in dark blue wool capes with peaked hoods; it ends at Piazza Trinità, with a mountain vista that makes you feel like the king of the world. Packed in between are a church; the town hall; a general store selling lace collars, toys and men's hats; and two bars with plate-glass windows lined with blue boxes of Perugina chocolates and dark-green bottles of Cynar, a bitter artichoke liqueur. The corso then had two butchers: one for beef and pork, one for poultry. The poultry butcher sold eggs on the side. I could buy just one egg if that's all I needed, and he would roll it up for me in a brown paper cone.

At that time, the corso also had two drugstores, one with an outdoor condom-vending machine dispensing four brands in assorted colors and prices. A greengrocer stacked crates of lacy green-topped carrots outside his closet-sized store. Municipal workers passed through the fifteen-foot carved double doors of the town hall, a three-hundred-year-old former Jesuit school. People wedged into and out of a glassed-in newsstand the size of two telephone booths to buy their weekly soccer lottery tickets. Pick the winners of thirteen games and you're a millionaire.

In the back streets the balconies were banked with geraniums—pink, red, and green. A stone cherub with fat cheeks spat water into a stone bowl under a tree outside the Pensioners' Club. Someone had left a courtyard gate ajar. I peeked in and saw a white stucco wall stained green with moss, and ornamental trees in pink terra-cotta pots. Someone had just watered them; the hose lay on the ground still leaking in the walled garden. I breathed in the elemental scent, a wash of water on stone. At a street fountain, a stone lion spewed an icy stream into a man's plastic jug. At the edge of town a cowherd drove his cows up out of the valley, their brass bells clanging deep and hollow.

The silvery mist thickened into a light rain. A woman leaned out her second-story window to pull in her laundry. A girl opened her front door to sweep out some dust. I saw her eyeing me through the crack before she quietly clicked the door shut. These streets were so close and intimate that I felt I'd walked into someone's stone boudoir. Every time I put my foot down, it rolled over the soft convex curve of a stone. Each one had passed through the hands of a builder who had felt its shape and heft before setting it in the mosaic. In the rain the stones shone like puffed satin pillows—uneven, imperfect, and of humans. Hand-painted pink ceramic placards named the cross street at every corner; house numbers appeared in smaller, matching pink tiles. Wrought-iron lamps curved out over the street. The people did this all for themselves, not for tourists. So high, so serene, so alone, this town. It hardly seemed real.

I trailed my fingers along the stone walls and felt the energy locked up in them, then I stood still for a minute and looked around me. This town felt like an old-growth forest: silent living things with deep roots. *Maybe this was what Santa Margherita was once. Maybe Nana grew up in a crystalline place like this.*

After a few days of commuting from Palermo with Joseph, I found an apartment in Polizzi for the rest of his assignment. I balked at the price tag of $250 for fifteen days. But when the owner turned the key in the lock, I walked straight through the yellow kitchen to the balcony door and sucked in my breath at what I saw. Snow-capped crags, peak behind peak, sheep grazing beside an eleventh-century church, the canyon, and the broad valley below. I was in one of those buildings flush with the cliff face. The apartment came with no heat, no

broom, no coffee pot, no dishes, and three stark, echoing bedrooms. I told the owner, "I'll take it."

Joseph brought his portable typewriter and wrote newspaper stories at the kitchen table at night. "Substitute teachers
don't usually get to see the towns they teach in," he said. "I
like this one." At seven every evening, a policeman set up
sawhorses at both ends of the corso to prohibit cars and the
people took back the street for an hour before supper. Every
night we walked arm in arm down the corso among all the
people in town. Joseph's students were surprised to see him
after school. We walked slowly over the smooth stones under
the curving lamps between the protective walls to Piazza
Trinità. Then we turned around and walked back again, greeting new friends, talking, making clouds with our breath.

To find out how Polizzi Generosa got its name, I started at the
library, which was then a dark, dank, high-ceilinged hall,
cold as a tomb. The librarian, Grazia Ortolano, stood in the
Dickensian chill presiding over two boys doing their homework. An electric heater glowed red under the table, and her
sons bent over their books with their coats on. When I asked
for a book on Polizzi's history, Grazia handed me a few vol-
umes and plugged in a second heater.

Historians have several theories about Polizzi Generosa's
name, but none has anything to do with generous policemen.
When the Normans came in the early eleventh century they
found a city called Basileopolis, "city of the king," which per-

sonally belonged to the Eastern Roman emperor, who had just fortified it against the Arabs. When the Norman conqueror, Roger I, took it he made it part of his personal demesne. The name Basileapolis may have changed through the years into Polizzi. Maybe. Some say that Polizzi is the namesake of the Palici gods, Castor and Pollux, in local legend the twin sons of the nymph Thalia, to whom a temple was dedicated near the town. "Palici" may have transformed into "Polizzi." Others say Polizzi was once the "Polis Iside," the "city of Isis," the Egyptian mother goddess.

About the year 1650, amazed townsmen pulled a life-sized sculpture from a deep well near the old Jewish baths. Carved of white marble, it was believed to be Isis-Minerva. Centuries earlier, villagers had probably hidden her in the well before an attack. The men who found her moved her into their cathedral, where she held up the holy water font until 1764, when workers began church renovations and moved the statue to a piazza. When repairs were done parishioners asked their resident bishop, Castelli, for permission to return Isis to the cathedral. Appalled by the idea of a pagan goddess in church, he not only refused permission but also had the statue smashed to bits by a Capucin monk whom he supplied with a sledgehammer. Forty-three men of the town's governing body, equally appalled by Castelli's lack of respect for the statue's antiquity, signed a letter of protest and sent it to their "superstitious" bishop. In it they included a sketch of Isis, "drawn from life," so that no one could say she never really existed. They described her in loving detail.

"This is what we know for certain, and saw with our own eyes," they wrote. She was of the whitest marble, her long hair hung loose over her shoulders and down her back. Three faces bloomed from her long neck. The one facing front was of a young woman. In the center of her forehead a flower bloomed inside a triangle, perhaps a symbol of the fertile Nile delta, which was her origin. Her left face was that of a bearded, wizened man, eyes open wide. Her right face was of an androgynous child. The figure of Isis held two snakes in her right hand, their heads reaching up toward the sash girdling her tunic. In her left hand she held a semispherical object, which could have been a globe, or a loaf of bread.

Isis was the protectress of the grain crops that had made Polizzi rich, the three-faced ruler of past, present and future, and of the three seasons of life: childhood, maturity, and old age. The people of Polizzi still mourned for her. I saw her framed image in their bars, stores, and offices nearly as often as I saw crucifixes.

Frederick II, the king of Sicily and *stupor mundi,* "wonder of the world," the great half-German, half-Sicilian Holy Roman emperor who made Palermo his capital, added the title "the Generous" to Polizzi's name in 1234 because of the town's generosity to his army when he fought wars in northern Italy and central Europe. To assure Frederick's victory and to retain its favored status as demesne of the king, Polizzi supplied him with more arms, men, horses, and grain than did Palermo, the seat of his empire. Polizzi became a proud town that bred a race of generous people. Their descendants now populated this village.

Here was an air of confident openheartedness, so different from xenophobic Santa Margherita, where Calogero had me cross the street for safety whenever he saw an unfamiliar face and where women on the town bus whispered behind me, "*Ma chista, cu è?*"—"But this one, who is it?" When, a lone stranger, I walked around in Polizzi, instead of suspicious looks people spontaneously offered me fruit, a calendar, a cookbook, a cup of coffee, vegetables from a wheelbarrow, three-course meals, and a place to warm myself out of the rain. This town, once nothing more to me than a curious name on a map, had opened up to me. I felt as though Isis had poured diamonds in my hands.

ॐ   ॐ   ॐ

I left Polizzi a day sooner than planned in order to get a lift from Joseph. His teaching job was over a day before my lease was up, and he had to be back in Santa Margherita, which was my destination, too. If I could pack in a hurry, I wouldn't have to lug everything on buses the following day. So I packed and we left and I whimpered all the way down the mountain. I didn't want to leave. I didn't have time to say goodbye to the lady in the apartment below mine. I had met her just once at our front door. She had smiled at me, amused, I think, and only said "Good day! Good day!" She never mentioned the panties she found impaled on her artichokes, and I never asked for them back.

11

FAVA BEANS

ॐ

JOSEPH BROUGHT ME BACK to Santa Margherita. After Nella's pasta-flinging incident I had taken to eating a brown-bag lunch in the park that had once been the Leopard's garden. But one day the iron gate was locked. Across the street from the entrance, at the bottom of a staircase, I saw a broad, spring-fed watering trough shaded by trees and choked with chartreuse algae.

I picked a spot on the ground with no ants or sheep dung next to the soothing splash of the stream. I took out my bread and cheese and the book I was reading and used my knapsack for a pillow. The book was *I Siciliani (The Sicilians)*, by the Catanian journalist Giuseppe Fava, who had written about the Mafia and was shot to death by them in 1984. I had just opened the book and leaned back to read when an old man on a mule came by.

The man let his mule drink from the trough while he filled his jug from the stream. I spied him over the top of my book but I had resolved not to commune with strangers here after the mattress man had followed me home. This elderly man appeared to be well into his seventies, with a white stubble on his hollow cheeks. He looked at me, munching and reading.

"Where are you from?" he asked. It was the thin edge of the wedge. His mule was well groomed, tall, brown, and furry.

"America," I said.

"What are you doing here?"

"My grandparents were born here."

"Who are they?"

I knew from experience he'd recognize their family nicknames, but not their Christian names.

"My grandfather was a Black Olive."

He didn't know any Black Olives. "My grandmother's mother was Mary, the Little Spoon."

"*Sì, sì,*" he knew a few Little Spoons, and he rattled off their names as he bent to fill his bottles.

"Where are you staying? Did you rent a house?"

Now he was getting personal. But I had a prim answer.

"I am staying with my lady cousin."

"Who would that be?"

I invoked Nella's name.

"Oh, yes." He was a distant relative of her father's. "Do you know her Uncle Stefano?" he asked. I didn't.

"How can you not know him? He has two daughters in America! One came back to Santa Margherita to get married. Are you married?"

"No."

"Why not?"

"Nobody wants me."

"How can that be? You're young and pretty."

Sure, I look good to you, I thought. *You're pushing eighty.*

He remounted, swinging his right leg over the bulky, handmade saddle, built on a wooden tree and padded with folded burlap bags. I could have cried for having lightened my pack by leaving my camera at home that day.

"See?" he said as he reined his mule toward a trail head. "We exchanged a few words and learned a lot about each other." I thought, *You know a lot about me; all I know about you is that you ride a handsome mule.* But then I thought, *Maybe I've become too suspicious.* When you travel alone, you have only yourself to argue with. He was leaving, his back to me, when I reclined on my makeshift pillow and picked up my book.

"*Ciao,*" I said.

He turned around. "I'll bring you some fava beans if you're still here when I get back. I'll be gone two or three hours." He turned his mule toward a hillside bean patch down the yellow dirt path bordered by eye-high purple thistles. I watched the mule's rump rise and fall with each plodding step. Just before he disappeared over the rise, the peasant twisted around in his saddle and said, "You can come if you like."

"No, thanks," I said, and immediately felt remorse. *You want to learn about mountain life yet you turn down an invitation to pick beans?* I thought. But in less than a minute, he returned. "Back so soon?" I asked. The old man didn't look at me, but at the ground. I thought he'd dropped something. But no. When he got behind the stone wall so nobody could see him or his mule from the road, he asked me simply, *"Vuole fare l'amore?"* In the politest of terms, he was asking me for sex.

I tried righteous indignation.

"Whatever are you thinking?" I asked him right back. I furrowed my brow to look offended. I had used the polite form, too. He reined his mule around.

"Just asking. Just a word. I won't mention it again." He held the palm of his hand toward me, as if to ward off my fury. He wasn't embarrassed at all.

I said, "How about a little respect?" He pretended not to hear or understand and ambled off to pick beans, happy as hell, I was sure, that he hadn't told me his name.

I gathered up my things with a new resolve not to speak to strangers, not even to men on mules.

When I told Nella what had happened, she said the watering trough was where the town prostitute worked.

12

CONTINUING EDUCATION

ॐ

Sicilian teachers and their students must grab what fate throws at them, or duck.

Marisa, a friend of mine in Santa Margherita and a teacher with two teenage children, told me the story of her first job. In Italy, public school teachers are employed by the federal government and guaranteed an assignment in their home province. Santa Margherita is in the province of Agrigento, which also includes Linosa, a tiny island off Sicily's southern coast halfway to Africa. Years before, with a new teacher's degree, a husband, and a three-year-old son, Marisa learned that Linosa was her first assignment. She found her courage, left her husband at his job, and took their son, Gaspare, to the island.

"From the ferry, it looked like a cork floating in a swimming pool," Marisa said. Linosa is so remote and hard to approach that the federal prison there has no walls. Other than prisoners, the inhabitants were fishermen and their families who lived in pastel-painted houses. As the ferry approached the island, Marisa was tempted to turn back. "But if I didn't take my first assignment I'd never get another job teaching," she said.

Competition for teaching jobs is so high in Sicily that I had met two women in two different towns who had taught in public schools for no pay. They had worked not for money but for "points" that would give them seniority, all else being equal, when they eventually applied for another teaching job elsewhere. Their principals had pocketed their salaries with the complicity of a friend at the bank who cashed the checks without asking questions, probably for a cut.

Marisa said the Linosa islanders treated her coldly, even though she was teaching their children, because she was a foreigner from the north. None of them would care for her son while she was at school, so she made friends with a prisoner, one who always wore a suit and never removed his sunglasses, and hired him to take care of little Gaspare.

"My baby-sitter was awaiting sentencing for murder," she said.

❧ ❧ ❧

One day in March when I was living in Polizzi, I walked to the high school to meet my cousin Joseph, the engineer and substitute teacher, for his eleven o'clock break. The school for architects' assistants, where Joseph was teaching, was housed in the old deconsecrated Church of Our Lady of Carmel. When I buzzed, the *bidella* opened the door. Her job title made her school housemother, concierge, sergeant-at-arms, and janitor. In a pinch she filled in for missing teachers. I was early, class wasn't out yet, so she took me straight to Joseph's classroom.

Outside it was cold, but the classroom was close and steamy with the mixed vapors of sweat and pheromones. Physical education was mandatory but the school had no shower rooms. The students—teenagers and twenty-somethings in jeans and Timberland boots—were more interested in each other than in Joseph's lesson. They opened the windows but the panes remained fogged. Joseph sat on a dais watching one boy chalk out a homework problem on the board. The crucified Christ hung above him. Officially, church and state are separated in Italy, but in Sicily Christ hangs in every post office, train station, school, and town hall. A benevolent chaos pervaded the room. Joseph rapped his knuckles on his desk and politely asked for quiet, which he got for three seconds. He did not expect miracles.

Joseph was not what they had hoped for in a substitute; he actually meant to teach them something. Their own professor had been gone for weeks; no one was really sure why, or when or whether he was coming back. Joseph had attended the same kind of high school, so he knew all the students' tricks. He gave two grades to cheaters: one for correct answers, one for quality of copying. Joseph got up and walked around the tables, offering help. One girl with frizzy hair in a ponytail—and a centered grace that made her as chic as any Parisian—wrinkled her nose at the problem at hand. "*Arabo*," she said to Joseph. Arabic, it was all Arabic to her, as it might have been all Greek to me.

The school was equipped with teachers, blackboards, and desks, nothing more. The students used their own pocket calculators. The school's only computer belonged to the secretary, and he brought it home every night. I saw no drafting tables, and the only sign of a science lab was a set of dusty glass test tubes in a cabinet in La Signorina's office.

That's where the teachers met for coffee and announcements at eleven. It was really the principal's office, but he was always at a sister school in Palermo, so his lieutenant, a short, stern, aging spinster called simply La Signorina, tried to run the place by the book. Joseph sweet-talked her into allowing me into the classroom with a camera. The geography teacher appeared with a tiny pot of espresso and poured three drops in everyone's outstretched paper cups.

La Signorina rapped a pencil on her desk, called for attention from her troupe of chatty teachers, made announcements, and fixed everybody's days off for the week. Teachers get Sunday off and one other free day of their choice. The class clown from Joseph's topography class came in with a cold bottle of spumante he had bought at the Bellavista Bar. There is no minimum drinking age in Sicily. Wine is food here, and no one intended to get drunk. He passed out the paper cups and poured a little wine for everybody, including a cup for himself. He toasted our health. Bottoms up. As far as I could see, all we were celebrating was the prolongation of the eleven o'clock break.

❧ ❧ ❧

In 1986, when I lived for a year in Mondello, near Palermo, with Piero, my fisherman boyfriend, he had paid for my Italian lessons with a kilo of fish. I remember the exchange, the weight of six dead mackerel swinging in a knotted plastic sack. "Feed them to your kids," Piero said when he handed the bag to his friend, Professore Michele LoMonaco, a gaunt but handsome middle-aged man who had never become the lawyer he had aspired to be. Instead he tutored children in his *doposcuola,* a private "after-school" where he taught them what they couldn't or wouldn't learn in public school. Michele's youngest pupil was a girl of eight and the oldest was sixteen, until I became a student again at thirty-three. I attended the less crowded day session.

Three mornings a week I walked the mile and a half from the Piazza Mondello to his school, one long, thin, bare room with no windows. The space felt like the inside of a giant compressor. A light bulb hung from a wire descending fifteen feet from the ceiling. A sticky strip spiraled down the wire, dotted with exoskeletons and desperate flies buzzing their last. We sat on wooden benches at two long wooden tables and wore our coats inside. At ten on sunny days in winter a ray of light burst through the transom and we shifted around to sit in the sunbeam. Michele multitasked, teaching subtraction to the eight-year-old girl, history to the ten-year-old boy, and English to the teenager. He started me with the ABC's.

For a few years the professor represented his borough, comprising Partanna and Mondello, on the Palermo city council. Since he was close to power, there was always some shadow at the door, a fellow citizen come to ask a favor, or a mother pleading with him to tutor her lazy son. When he stepped across the street to consult with a supplicant at his brother's café, he always left me in charge to prevent mayhem.

Italians place great emphasis on oral presentation; style earns more points than substance. Once Professore Michele had his history student stand up before the class for an oral quiz. The professor sat at the room's back wall. When the boy stammered and hesitated, Michele leaned forward and flung the five-pound book across the room. I remember its long overhead arc. The boy ducked; the book hit the door. When Michele yelled, it was in Sicilian, but I think he told him to study harder.

I proceeded through dictations, pronunciation (I never did get the double consonants right), all the tests in a fifth-grade Italian grammar text, and six hours of homework a week. From a sixth-grade history book I gained an understanding of the feudal underpinnings of Sicilian culture. I conjugated verbs in all the moods and most of the tenses. I increased my vocabulary by reading *L'Ora*, Palermo's now-defunct afternoon paper, aloud. In a couple of months I could speak without having to mentally translate first. One morning I woke and remembered that I had dreamed in Italian, a milestone in learning a new language.

After three months the professor gave me written assignments. In my first essay I was to address myself to Mondello's problems and list my solutions for them. I spent six hours at

Piero's kitchen table and came up with more problems than solutions: petty crime at the beach, pollution of Mondello Bay, and the stench of uncollected garbage outside seafood restaurants, among others. I handed in my homework. The next time I saw it, it was on the front page of a monthly newspaper, *Mondello Cultura e Sport*, edited by Michele LoMonaco. For ensuing issues, the professor gave me all of Page Three, the lifestyle section. So when school let out for summer my education continued on the street.

I had fun. I filled Page Three with man-on-the-street polls; interviews with fishermen-philosophers and local painters, poets, and lifeguards; travel stories from my jaunts around the island; and photographs of the kids' street soccer teams.

A group of local businessmen had put up the seed money for the paper, but it needed advertising revenue. So Michele made me the sales department and said I could keep ten percent of what I grossed. I sold ad space in Palermo the way I used to sell Girl Scout cookies in New Jersey—door-to-door, a crazy idea that worked.

It meant I could quit my job teaching English at the "British Institute" in Palermo, where Signore Castagna, my Sicilian boss, warned me never to tell his students I was not born in England. "Mr. Chestnut" ran this private school in a few rooms on swank, tree-lined Via Libertà. He paid his instructors a pittance—usually late—and fobbed me off as a Brit. He gave me Oxford University textbooks to teach from; I made *brutta figura* every time I had to leave my class to ask him what some word meant in British English. My students paid good money but they never studied, hoping that they would just catch English from me, like a virus. Mr. Chestnut still owes me one hundred fifty dollars.

My newspaper sales pitch was paying off; I had lots of orders. I designed the ads myself, even used my own drawings. Getting paid was harder, and Michele now made it clear to me that I was also the billing and collections departments. But in his humble school, for a sack of fish, the professor had taught me enough Italian to convince Sicilians to cough up what they owed, and I spent my ten percent commission on bus tickets to small mountain towns.

13

ZAFFERANA ETNEA

❧

It was May 1992, and Etna was erupting in a spectacular fashion. Each night we watched on Nella's television as a river of orange rock raged down its invisible slopes. We saw the explosions at the summit and the red lava dripping like candle wax down the smooth shoulder of the mountain. Zafferana Etnea was the town most threatened by the awesome flow.

"Are you afraid?" a reporter asked an altar boy. That day, the parishioners had paraded the statue of the Madonna and Child through town to plead for heavenly help. The boy, still in his white alb, was just leaving an all-night vigil held in a makeshift church under a tent they'd been using since their own church had cracked in an 1980's earthquake.

"If we were afraid, we wouldn't live here," the boy said.

The scene switched to a shrine on the edge of town, where another lava flow from another century had stopped miraculously and cooled. We watched American helicopters from Sigonella, the NATO naval base in Catania, bombing the volcano to divert the flow, but it didn't work. Their next plan was to staunch the flow by dropping house-sized cement blocks in a narrow gorge, thus plugging the valley. Meanwhile, four local heroes with a backhoe were digging a diversion canal in the hellish lower stretches of the lava flow, working under the direction of Zafferana's mayor. One man hosed down the backhoe bucket so it wouldn't melt while they dug.

All the action was on the eastern side of the island. I borrowed a sleeping bag and the next morning before dawn I took the bus to Palermo, then another to Catania, about twenty-five miles south of Zafferana Etnea. As soon as I got off the coach I asked an off-duty driver if there was a local bus to Zafferana, on the southeast slope of the volcano.

"Follow me," he said. "You want to see the lava?" He was the driver and he was leaving immediately. "You were born with your shirt on." That means you're lucky, to be born with clothes on your back.

It was a happy bus. People in the towns we went through flagged it down just to talk to passengers they knew. The conductor who punched tickets let one girl ride for free with a promise that she'd pay next time. At the higher elevations the houses were made of lava block, the inky black contrasting beautifully with the orange roof tiles. Etna stood silhouetted in the distance, a gray triangle with its pointed peak blown off. By midafternoon I came face to face with my first lava flow.

I began to walk uphill and asked the way to the action. The Italian army had set up security checks on the road leading to the flow. Besides official vehicles, only journalists could pass. I flashed them my out-of-date *Brattleboro Reformer* press pass, which sufficed. The army boys had commandeered an entire apartment building and said if I couldn't find a hotel room I could come back and stay with them. They seemed to be in a party mood.

I asked, "Why are all of you here?"

"We're here to stop the lava," one guard said. He paused a beat, then laughed. It was absurd, and everybody knew it.

I hiked the mile and a half to the lowest point of the lava flow, passing through stone-terraced vineyards that produce a wine as black as the soil it grows in, and green hills dusted with huge, hot-pink clover buds. I had never seen cooling lava and didn't know what to look for. A full moon rose over the snowy mountain peak. Near dusk I turned into the field where twisted old grapevines were putting forth their first green shoots. Peach and pear trees planted between the vines were covered in soft pink and white blossoms. It looked like a Japanese woodcut. I heard a soothing, crackling fire and saw a group of people.

The warmth I felt as I approached them was no campfire but the face of the lava flow. People had gathered in a semi-circle before it. After four months it had finally reached this little orchard, having crept down five miles from a hole that gushed magma at thirty cubic yards per second. Close to its source, the lava was a glowing red river of fire. But here, five miles from the fissure, the lava had cooled to about 1,872 degrees Fahrenheit. It now crept forward a foot and a half per hour, and would stop only when it cooled another 800 degrees. What it had lost in speed it gained in height: here in Giuseppe Fichera's vineyard, the lava was twenty feet high and nearly a hundred yards across. I stood ten feet from the lava wall—any closer and I would have roasted. All was quiet. I joined the people who faced the living lava and murmured among themselves.

First I saw its cooling, rounded skin, all black. Then the tiny veins of red, molten rock glowing through cracks in the crust. Then I heard the crinkling of tissue paper, then porcelain shattering into shards. It was the flow inching forward, shedding its crust. Slowly it crushed grapevines, smothered fruit trees, engulfed a farm house. It bulged and swallowed the trunk of a pear tree in flower. Sometimes, Fichera said, a tree would explode when its sap superheated. Fichera and his wife watched the black worm slowly consume their crop. It was not the first time. You can buy postcards of Etna farmers watching their crops burn. "This field won't produce again for another five hundred years," he said.

It was dark when I got back to town, and every hotel room was filled with reporters from as far away as Sweden, the United States, and Japan. I went to the police station to see if I could curl up in my sleeping bag on a pew in the church. The lady who cleaned the police station gave me the keys instead to an apartment she wasn't using. She understood my fascination with the lava flow and didn't want me to miss it.

I stayed a couple days in Zafferana Etnea. The mountain was still erupting when I packed up. The bus I left town on pulled over and stopped to let a caravan of Italian army trucks pass in the narrow street. They were loaded with soldiers who waved and smiled at our bus. They looked like college kids in uniform on spring break. I saw them again on Nella's television. After a few days, Etna went back to sleep; the creeping flow cooled and stopped, the soldiers went back to meaningful work, and the film crews packed their cameras, while stupefied farmers, who had to start over or leave, stared at their fields and scratched their heads.

14

BORGO CATENA

⊰⊱

Franco D'Amico milked 180 ewes and made ricotta cheese the old-fashioned way. His farm was a collection of house, sheds, and stone barns in the village of Borgo Catena, thirty miles north of Zafferana Etnea and a half-hour walk from Linguaglossa, on the northeast side of Etna. A stand of pines rose behind Franco's house, which looked like a Swiss chalet made of varnished pine boards. A small vineyard grew beside it and prickly pears sprouted wild around the walls with here and there a palm or a wild olive. Hard green oranges hung from a tree in his door yard, where chickens pecked between the paving stones.

The sheep, of no particular breed, were penned and guarded by an untrained shepherd mutt who felt proprietary. The dog followed Franco and his flock as they wandered Etna's lower slopes. The volcano shaped their world. Everything Franco saw originated from it—the hills and ridges, the streets, the buildings, the grass that his sheep ate, and the soil it grew in. He owned some mountain pastures, and paid for grazing rights on the land of others. I saw no stock fences, only the low walls made of lava chunks, no obstacle for sheep or the few goats that traveled with them. The mountain's smooth cone breathed white steam into their sky all day and the landscape under it was all cooled lava.

"We have had no earthquake here," said Franco's wife, Lucia. "But the lava covers everything—the houses, the land. When the lava comes, you try to save what you have inside. The house, you can't do anything to move it. But the furniture, everything inside, you can remove. At least you can save that. Because if you don't, everything goes under."

"And you don't think of living elsewhere?" I asked.

"We were born here," she said. "We feel safe."

Lucia Raiti, her sister-in-law, said, "There are dangers anywhere you go. Here the problem is Etna but in other places there are other dangers. Floods. Hurricanes. We feel just fine here. We aren't afraid of staying here, not at all."

Lucia D'Amico's mother, uncles, and aunts had had to flee during the lava flow of 1923. "They had a little hazelnut orchard, and Etna put it under." Like my old Zia Betta, they live as God wills.

It was ten o'clock in the morning on a Sunday and Lucia led me to a windowless shed constructed of lava blocks. We stepped onto a dirt floor in a dark, quiet room where time slowed to the rhythm of dripping milk, breath, and crackling flames. Franco milked twice a day. Ninety liters of ewe milk simmered in a cast-iron cauldron hanging from a hook above the fire. Franco stirred with a long wooden spoon while his father split wood. "Our sheep make little milk because we don't give them any grain, but the milk is fattier. Grain-fed sheep give more milk, but their milk has less fat and produces less ricotta."

As the cauldron steamed and the smell of hot sheep's milk curled through the room, Franco's clients arrived in their church clothes. Everyone knew Franco's hours and had standing orders. Seven or eight people—men in suits, women in furs—stared at the pot on the fire. Lucia disappeared then came back with soup spoons and bowls of yellow bread broken up into chunks. We each took a bowl and stood around expectantly. Franco's father fed twigs to the fire.

While we waited for the curds, Lucia led me to her store room to see the wheels of salted ricotta and pecorino shot with whole peppercorns aging on shelves. She showed me the woven cheese forms made of *ungo*, a grass that grows in Sicilian rivers. "The deeper the water, the taller and more robust the grass grows," Lucia said. "Men go and choose the best of these, then weave them into these forms." The rivers are shallow now; the grass and the men who collect it are scarce. "The forms are very expensive," she said. "It's another trade that is being lost. When you buy cheese at the market and it has the impressions of this woven basket on it, you know you have bought a local cheese made with pure ingredients, the old-fashioned way."

Back in the room with the steaming cauldron, a man was saying, "The European Union is going to kill the craftsmen." He had brought his young daughter to see the cheese made.

"The health inspectors have been watching us since January," Franco said. "They want us to cook with gas. And this we don't want."

"Why is gas preferred?" I asked.

"The smoke from the wood pollutes the air, they say," Franco said. "Money rules. If you ask me, they want to put us out of business." He felt the European Union favored milk from sanitized, industrial dairies in France, Holland, and Belgium.

Another older man entered the dark congregation and Franco greeted him: *"Zu Francesco! Buon giorno."* Then he continued: "I was at a farm in Sweden where I saw one person, ONE person, handle two hundred fifty cows." The dairyman could feed, milk, and sell to restaurants all by himself. But his were purebred cows that gave sixty liters of milk a day, and every one of them had a computer attached to it, Franco said. "How are we supposed to compete with that?"

Franco's sheep were a bastard breed but they were survivors and all Sicilian. Grazing free under the Etna sky, they ate only what the mountain gave them and made cream of it.

The cheese was ready. Franco's father ladled ricotta into every outstretched bowl, smothering the bread with hot curds and whey. Lucia held out a palmful of crunchy salt and we each sprinkled a pinch on our breakfast. We took our steaming bowls outside and held them under our chins and ate blinking in the sun with the smell of sheep manure in our nostrils. The ricotta and bread went down hot and sustaining, mountain food potent enough to keep one from going under.

15

THE CYCLE OF BREAD

࿐

In Santa Margherita's birth records, written on parchment in faded brown ink in florid European script, the occupation of all my Sicilian male ancestors is listed as *villano*, which means peasant or country person but which also means boor or uncouth person. While the Leopard's life took place in the upper rooms of Palermo bordellos, or in second-floor ballrooms in palazzos, or in his rooftop observatory, the life of the common man was earthbound, tied to the streets and fields, and the lives of the women were bound to the home and church. The peasant farmers plowed, planted, watered, weeded, and harvested the wheat, grapes, and olives, kept livestock and made cheese. The women helped harvest, then turned the wheat to bread, the olives to oil, the tomatoes to paste. They shopped and sold at market and ruled the courtyards and water fountains, where lines were long, tempers flared, and best friends got into fights if one of them tried to cut in.

Into the 1950's the mayor would send the town crier around with edicts from town hall: "Clean up after your animals. Don't leave your donkey dung in the street." Wheat was the currency in Santa Margherita through the 1950's, when the fiscal year still ended September fourth, after the grain was harvested, threshed, measured, and stored. All year long when a man got his hair cut or his shoes resoled, the merchant would take a small knife from his pocket and nick the dry yucca stalk where he kept the man's account. In September his client would pay his bills in flour or grain.

I had hoped to find in the birth records some hint that I could be the product of a "prima nox," a baron's right to spend the first night with all the brides of his realm. If a woman protested that she was married, the baron might hang her husband and make her a widow. I traced my grandfather's line back to 1699 but none of my ancestors was illegitimate, which would have been noted as "found on the wheel." The wheel was a revolving shelf in the orphanage wall where children born out of wedlock, or to families too poor to care for them, could be placed anonymously at night. The child was spun around into the care of nuns, who would name the child and raise it.

For forty years in the early 1800's, Rosalia Armato was the town's busiest midwife and the orphanage's official "receiver," so she probably knew when a baby was about to be deposited, and whose child it was. She would round up the required two godparents and have the child baptized with the name of the patron saint of the day. (All Italian calendars give this information.) For a surname, these babies were often given family names from out of town, according to the town clerk who helped me decipher the writing. An out-of-town name would mark the child for life, and make her suffer for the sin of her parents.

In Rome, I am told, when the nuns filled out a foundling's birth certificate they filled in the blank after "mother" with the words "M. *Ignota*" for *madre ignota*, "mother unknown." With the addition of a *t* the word became *mignotta*, Roman slang for a prostitute. In Naples, the nuns wrote *"esposito,"* from the Latin for "from this place," for an abandoned child. In other towns, when asked the child's family name, the nuns might fill in the blank with *"Diolosà,"* "God knows it" or *"D'Angelo,"* "from the angel."

Legitimate children in Santa Margherita were named according to a strict protocol—the first son after his paternal grandfather, second son after the maternal grandfather, first daughter after the paternal grandmother, second daughter after the maternal grandmother. Many first cousins had the same first and last names, which is why family nicknames like my own "Black Olive," *Pasaluna*, came in handy.

I opened the soft brown leather-bound book for the births in 1854, and turned to the index. Written in a spidery script, the index was in alphabetical order, but by first name, so that all the Marias were listed together, and all the Stefanos. The system made sense in this isolated town where there were more first names than surnames.

Vita Mauceri was born in 1854, an only child. Her mother died when she was two. Nobody knows why her father didn't leave her with relatives when he went to work in his fields. Instead he dressed her as a boy, protected her from the eyes of men, and kept her at his side until she began to grow breasts. Then he took her to the town convent where the nuns would keep her safe. There she met the gardener, the only man around, and married him. One of her sons was my grandfather, Papa.

꿏 꿏 꿏

One evening in Santa Margherita I found myself at an impromptu dinner party with Salvatore Armato, a man who had farmed all his life, and his wife, Calogera Nieli, who knew how to remove the Evil Eye. Everybody talked at once; the din echoed off the walls. Salvatore Armato was lean, spare, and animated. Life to him was the grain crop that dominated the interior valleys. When I asked him to tell me about life before the earthquake he stood up and took the floor. The chattering ceased; everyone wanted to hear again the story of the cycle of bread.

While the rich danced in the Leopard's garden and the prince ate eels from his fountain, this is how it was for the common man in Santa Margherita up until fifty years ago. "In December, men sowed wheat," Armato said. They pinched the seed between thumb and forefinger from a sack slung about their necks, lifting one arm in an arc above their heads. Armato showed us the motion. It looked like a gesture of defiance.

As soon as the seed was in the ground the farmer designated to pray would ask God to send a gentle rain. The peasants and their wives went to Mass twice a day to beg for the grain to grow. "We had no technology, so we used religion. We prayed, 'Dear Lord, let it rain, let it rain. The grain is dying of thirst. Give us a good one, with no lightning and no thunder.'" (According to Armato, at two-thirty in the afternoon, June 21, 1946, lightning killed two people and four animals.)

In those days, Armato said, the Most Holy Crucifix was carried through town three times a year, first to beg for rain, then in April to pray for warm sun, and on May 3 to celebrate the Crucifix's own feast day. In June they harvested the grain and tied the stalks into sheaves and carried them to the threshing house, where they spread them to dry in a circle twelve yards wide. A span of mules, or a horse and a mule, were yoked together and as many as three pairs simultaneously trampled the stalks. The grain dropped to the floor while the straw stayed on top. They trotted in one direction for three quarters of an hour. When the mules were knee-deep in straw, the driver called them by name and they stopped and rested twenty minutes before trotting around the other way. Armato sang us the mule driver's song.

When it was time to winnow they prayed to Saint Mark, patron saint of the wind, for a breeze to blow away the chaff. They piled the grains in the center of the circle. They swept the threshing floor and saved single grains by dropping the sweepings into a bucket of water where the wheat floated and the dirt sank. "And when we went to bed that night, we prayed that the ants didn't carry the harvest away," Armato said.

16

SICILIAN BAGPIPES

୬୨

SICILY STILL HAS PLACES where shepherds play bagpipes for the birth of Christ. One evening in Catania's Via Etnea, outside the bright shops under the Christmas lights, I heard a man in his twenties play. He'd come down from the mountain to play an instrument of the same type that Roman troops introduced to Scotland. He was absorbed in his breathing and the fingering of his apricot-wood pipe. The ribbons attached to it rose, fell, and fluttered in time with the tune. Mothers shopping with children stopped still around him, mesmerized by a sound that vibrated in their foreheads and chests. He wore an anachronistic outfit of soft boots, fleece pants, a woolen vest, and a tasseled hat with its long peak pulled before his right shoulder. He came from Maletto, the highest town on the volcano, where shepherds still play for the nine days before Christmas, and he was one of the last of his kind.

I'd been to Maletto, a rocky, windswept eyrie on Etna's north flank—one of those Sicilian towns that turns its back on the sea. In the middle ages it belonged to the Spadafora family; their castle was destroyed by a World War II bomb. Once in the summer I took the train there to hear a shepherd play, but the stationmaster said that all the shepherds were in the fields. At a café I learned of a retired shepherd and found him at his home. He showed me his bagpipe but he wouldn't play. "There is too much humidity; the pipes will be out of tune," he said. I didn't know then that they only play before Christmas. So in December I went back to try again. This time I was looking for Nunzio Putrino, the grand old man of Sicilian bagpipers, who lived at Il Pizzo, the highest point in town. The climb was steep and long; the street stones were rectangular and blue. Each time I got to a landing, I turned around to look behind me at blue and gray clouds scudding over green meadows below the train tracks, blotching the landscape with their streaming shadows.

Putrino's whitewashed house was set among white rocks at the end of a dirt path where the mountain pastures begin. I caught my breath and knocked on the door. Agata Messina, Putrino's wife, invited me in for coffee. I put my coat in the sitting room, where it was frosty, and took a seat at the kitchen table near the wood stove. She closed the door between the two rooms and hovered in her slippers behind her husband.

He was seventy-eight years old, broad in the chest and shoulders, imposing even seated at table. His hair was white and short-cropped, his face hard and angular. He wore a tan corduroy vest and brown corduroy pants and already had his instrument in his arms. I recorded his breaths as they filled the bag, which was the belly and legs of a giant ram he had bred, pastured, slaughtered, and skinned. He pressed the inflated hide to his chest and they held each other in a lover's embrace. He fixed me with his eyes, put his thick fingers on the flute, squeezed the bag, tuned the pipes with a little pink wax, and blew a medley of six pieces—"The Litany," "The Pastorale," "You Come Down from the Stars," "Bambolo," "I Love You," "The Bassadiera"—and his eyes never left mine. Each song he played came louder and faster. This instrument was never meant to be cooped up in a room; it overcame the senses and made me half dizzy. The hair stood up on my arms. I cringed under his piercing gaze and wrote useless notes to avoid it, but whenever I looked up he was still staring.

For thirty years Nunzio Putrino had played the nine nights before Christmas in Catania. Before the train tracks were laid on Etna's slopes, the Maletto bagpipers walked fifty miles to the city to earn a large part of their yearly income.

"In the old days we would play two hundred times a day, from four-thirty in the morning until ten-thirty at night. We had the same clients every year," Putrino said. The shepherds would go to the homes of city dwellers—aristocracy and working class alike—where they were invited to play before the living-room crèche. The family gathered around for this tradition; the pipes in a high-ceilinged vaulted room must have been thrilling. Putrino would play for three minutes, would accept a brandy against the cold, and was off to the next client. He made his rounds for the next eight days; on

Christmas Eve, each family gave him five lire. "Now they pay a hundred thousand lire [about 50 dollars]," Putrino said. "Fifty years ago five lire was worth more than a hundred thousand today."

"What kinds of work have you done in your life?" I asked him.

"I've been a farmer. And shepherd. A builder. I made my own house."

"We are great-grandparents," his wife, Agata Messina, said.

"Agata is a Catanian name," I remarked.

"I was born in Acireale and grew up in Catania," she said.

"How did you meet?" I asked, surprised their paths had crossed. The distant city was a world away.

Agata's father had hired Putrino to play in their living room every year. One Christmas, when Agata had grown into a pretty sixteen-year-old, Nunzio took his place before her family's crèche, fixed her with his eyes, and played. If she looked back, she was his.

"We never exchanged a word," she said. "He did it with his eyes, and I responded with mine." She was a well-bred city girl already engaged to another man, and Nunzio was a ruddy shepherd from the mountain. "But we fell in love," she said, which was a problem. The solution was a *fuitina*, a Sicilian way to bend the rules in one's favor. "We made our escape on the twenty-sixth and slept at his mother's house that evening." Whether or not she was still a virgin, her reputation had been ruined and now Putrino had to marry her as a point of honor. "We got married on February twenty-second," Agata said. Under the circumstances they had to exchange vows in the sacristy, not at the altar, and the bride could not wear white. But love triumphed and she got her man.

"I have ten children, seven girls and three boys," Nunzio Putrino said. "Not one of them plays. Not even the grand-children, and I have fifty-three."

17

THE ETNA LINE

ॐ

ON THE EAST COAST OF SICILY the little Etna train chugs seventy miles through some of the most spectacular scenery on the island, with the volcano as the centerpiece of every run. I've made the trip in every season and never needed a destination to ride; the Etna train is a linear world of its own. I would pay my ticket and board the orange car in Catania, a city of some 35,000. It made three stops in Catania to pick up shoppers and students, then headed to the edge of town past the junk piles, construction sites, and rusted cars into the citrus groves north of the city. And there it would be, a single blue mountain frosted with white and blowing a banner of steam.

Mount Etna started out as an eruption under the Ionian Sea a half million years ago. With its peak now 10,824 feet above sea level, the broad gentle slopes of its lower skirts form most of the eastern third of Sicily. The circumference of its base is eighty-seven miles. The Etna train runs through twenty-nine volcano towns, where every stationmaster tends a rose garden around his trim pink depot. Designed a century ago by an Englishman, Robert Trewheller, the narrow-gauge Ferrovia Circumetnea nearly circles the mountain, from Catania northwest and inland, around the mountain to Riposto, on the coast about ten miles north of Catania.

Now it's a passenger line, but the train once also hauled cargo and brought a measure of prosperity and culture to the high country by linking farmers to markets and students to the University of Catania. During World War II bombardments, many city dwellers escaped on the train to the relative safety of the mountain. Now the FCE also runs buses with air conditioning and cushioned seats, but the orange trolley remains a sentimental favorite. Farmers still set their watches by its screechy toot.

One December day I boarded the train to head up the mountain for a joyride. The filtered winter light made the colors glow in the citrus groves: Bright-yellow lemons bent their branches to earth, but the oranges were still hard green golf balls. Prickly pears grew wild along the tracks, their unripened fruit red, orange, and yellow. The sea glinted steel gray below us.

To me, small is beautiful. This train is never more than three cars long, so the atmosphere on board is informal. One time an engineer braked to a stop so I could get the perfect shot of a villa at the end of a cypress-lined lane. Once I got off at Maletto and left my notebook on my seat. It went to Riposto and came back on the noon train, whose conductor handed it to the Maletto stationmaster who summoned his nephew to find me in town. Once I missed my stop and the conductor let me ride for free to Riposto and back. "What were you going to do in Linguaglossa anyway?" he asked. "Relax and enjoy the ride."

On this trip we made an unscheduled layover at the Misterbianco station bar. When the engineer invited passengers for an espresso, nobody seemed surprised. I took him up on his offer. I had to laugh when I read the timetable: arrivals and departures were scheduled to the half minute.

Back en route, I knocked on the engineer's door. Carmelo Pace, middle-aged, bald, wearing sunglasses, let me in. His instrument panel was fitted in brass and steel. Through his windshield I could see the onrushing country. The vegetation changed as we circled and climbed: Below Adrano grew oleasters, the wild olives needed to fertilize cultivated ones; at Bronte grew pistachio nuts in plantations; at Maletto the crops were grains and beans and the country was very green. "No need for irrigation here," Carmelo said. "Just the water that falls from the sky." Giovanni Calì, the conductor, joined us and closed the door. Both of their grandfathers had worked for the FCE. "Winter is the best," Giovanni said. "When snow covers the tracks, it becomes a wonderland."

I asked them about the dangers they had encountered.

"Sheep," Carmelo said. They lined the track in spots and looked like rocks until they moved. "And people out for a walk." Twenty years ago, a mother and her children just back from picking wild greens had been squashed when they followed the tracks through a dark train tunnel. We came to a curve in the tracks, and a black rock. "Here there was a suicide." He pointed to the rock face. "He was right here." The man had lain down on the tracks and chosen the engineer for his executioner. Carmelo kept a holy card of Christ crucified taped to the windshield, next to a sticker of the Virgin, with the prayer "Oh, Mary, conceived without sin, pray for us."

At three thousand feet the land becomes a blackened moonscape and the tracks sink into a narrow channel chiseled through a century-old lava flow whose walls rise above the windows of the train. "In a hundred years, grass will grow here," Carmelo said. The first plant to grow back after an eruption is the broom, a yellow flower called *spaccapietra*, "the rock splitter," whose roots crumble stone and make soil as they seek water. It was growing all over, the bright life colors of yellow and green, stark and glowing against the lava.

The train cut through pastures and backyards where women hung their wash. I could hear church bells chime the hour. Men huddled in coats and scarves and played cards in the sunshine. A woman wiped her hands on her apron before stretching a chain barrier across a road. The FCE paid several people to block the crossing several times a day. "It's her husband's job," Carmelo said, "but he's off in the fields plowing."

As we pulled into Maletto a woman stepped out on the second-floor balcony over the tracks and stood behind the white sheet she was hanging. "That's my wife," Carmelo said as we passed under her feet. "Now when I get home she'll ask me, 'Who was that woman on the train?'" Outside Randazzo the seeking, curling tendrils of grapevines reached for the train as it passed through tidy vineyards. I would be getting off in Linguaglossa, the next town. From there to Riposto the train would coast down a steep slope bordered by long grasses and swaying palms.

Carmelo used to be a mechanic for the railroad, but switched to driving years ago. "Do you like this better?" I asked

"*Sì!*" he said. "It's more beautiful, you have more sensations. I have learned many things on the Circumetnea."

So had I.

While waiting for the train I learned that in October, hail the size of golf balls had fallen on the volcano vineyards. "Three hailstones together weighed a kilo," my fellow passenger said. "Thank God the grapes had been harvested." I learned that in Randazzo that summer the temperature had reached 115 degrees at four one afternoon. That it didn't rain from March until September. That the grass didn't grow so the sheep were thin and gave little milk, so the price of pecorino cheese was high. That those who had springs on their property had managed to save their strawberry crops. That the North African rug merchants who rode the rails with their wares on their shoulders felt the cold and sent money back to their mothers.

18

LINGUAGLOSSA

꩜

THE INNKEEPER WELCOMED ME and gave me my old room at the Villa Refe in Linguaglossa, my favorite town on Etna's northeast slope. She thought it strange that I slept with my shutters open—especially in winter—but that night the moon was full and closer to the earth than it would be for the next 130 years. It floated beside the volcano, tinted the snow blue, and canceled the stars. In the morning I always found fruit on my windowsill—plums in summer; now clementines, a gift from the volcano. I peeled one and looked at Etna. Some mornings she pulled charcoal-blue clouds over her head and dimmed the lights. Sometimes she woke chipper, all azure sky and new snow. Etna's mood shaped everyone's day.

That morning Etna wanted twilight all day. The sun filtered evenly through thin clouds and cast no shadows, a good day to photograph the *centro storico*, the old town split by Via Mareneve, "Sea and Snow Street," just a few blocks downhill from the train station. Hardly anyone is left in the old town now.

The houses are small, one room per floor, their walls made of black lava chunks the size of melons chinked with broken orange roof tiles. Their well-matched matte textures made me want to touch the stones and tiles; they held the warmth of the winter sun. Some facades are plastered smooth in baked earth tones and pastels—rusted orange, ashen pink, a cold periwinkle blue. The stucco is made from earth pigments mixed with powdered lava, which is what gives the colors their toasted hue. As time crumbles the plaster and peels away layers, the colors mix and swirl like an impressionist's palette. White limestone arches cap the wooden doors, all bolted with rusty brown hand-forged padlocks.

Etna was in the throes of a damp, cold depression, and the old center's streets were empty. Two thousand years ago Linguaglossa may well have been a bustling commercial lumber center where both Latin and Greek were spoken, for its name is made up of both languages' words for "language." The town is built just below an ancient Etna pine forest where the Greeks cut tall timbers for their shipyard at Naxos, their first Sicilian settlement, not far from Taormina, on the eastern coast. In Sicilian dialect, Linguaglossa means "fat tongue," which could refer to the tongue of lava the town was built on. Eruptions threaten it constantly. In the 1980's, lava covered the train tracks and crushed the vineyards between Linguaglossa and Randazzo. At the center of town a statue of Sant'Egidio, its chief patron saint, now stands atop a centuries-old lava flow that he is said to have stopped by brandishing his bishop's crook at the volcano.

In a deserted street where moss grew on the black stone wall and grass sprouted between the paving stones, I heard a piano and paused to listen outside a door. The music stopped. Whoever had been playing had heard my footsteps, or felt my presence; in this quiet, either was possible. A man opened the door, invited me in, and set a chair for me near his baby grand.

He was a composer, in his forties, and his family was among the last to live in the old center. He'd been commissioned to write a score and he was working it out. The tune was sweet and sad. It could have been the score for a movie made about this damp, lonely day on the north side of Etna. "The old fade away," the musician said. "The newlyweds take apartments on the edge of town. Everyone else has emigrated."

I didn't stay long. When I stepped out into the street he closed his door quietly and didn't play again for a few minutes. I walked deeper into the stone maze, an old town where people live in lava houses and shake sticks at the volcano. When I was blocks away the music began again—the heavyhearted notes he channeled from his mountain muse.

19

CHRISTMAS AT MALETTO

ॐ

Nunzio Putrino the bagpiper wasn't the only man I met in Maletto. The owner of Bar La Fragola told me, "You should meet my brother. He's a *fantasista.*"

"What's that?" I asked.

"A person with a big imagination and dreams." After a while his brother came in with his trench coat collar pulled up against the stinging rain and wind.

"It might snow," he said, and hung his coat and hat on a peg.

Maurizio Cutraro was in his late thirties, a self-styled impresario who managed song, dance, and magic acts, a one-man employment agency for the pretty and talented on this side of the volcano. His latest idea was to import reindeer to Sicily for Christmas pageants. He had driven a truck six days and nights to Finland to buy a small herd of reindeer for about ten thousand dollars, he said, and had trained them to pull a plywood "sleigh" through small villages on the volcano.

Municipalities paid him to bring Santa Claus to town. I arrived in Maletto one morning just to see this.

The parade formed just above the train station. Santa Claus walked beside the sleigh in an ill-fitting beard and a red suit trimmed with white. A reindeer the size of a Great Dane was trying to buck and burst free, but Santa kept a firm grip on its antlers. Three long-legged Santa Clausettes in black boots and red miniskirts marched on and a couple of Maletto's young bagpipers brought up the rear, piping Santa into town. They turned into the school playground, where the mayor was supposed to make a speech at ten.

The little reindeer was hyperventilating, its untrimmed hooves splayed on the asphalt, its heaving flanks steaming, its eyes bulging with fear, held immobile by Santa's heavy hand. All the screaming children wanted to touch its antlers. One gave it the finger.

I walked into the school where a clown twisted balloons into animal shapes for shrieking kids. The teachers were smoking in the hallway. The custodian told me I ought to take a picture of the beautiful crèche, and then asked to see my written permission to take photos in the school. Then he decided I'd better wait outside. I watched in the playground while the children were let out in small groups to harass the reindeer.

I left before the mayor showed up. And before Maurizio could make his next dream come true: importing dromedary camels from Tunisia. "They'd make a fine Epiphany scene," he said.

20

LA PIOVRA

ॐ

SICILIANS THEMSELVES SAY their island would be heaven on earth if it weren't for the Sicilians. They are only half joking. The Mafia, a Sicilian institution, is behind many of their daily aggravations. The Mafia's cruelty for cruelty's sake, its quest for power and money through any means, and the fear it engenders are suffocating, oppressive, and ubiquitous.

The year I lived in Mondello, near Palermo, I asked a French girlfriend, the wife of a Palermo city councilman, why I had to dodge so much dog dirt on the city's sidewalks. "Why don't they pass a law to make owners clean it up?" I asked Annie.

"There is a law," she said.

"Why don't they enforce it?"

"Because if a policeman sees a lady in a fur coat walking her poodle, he doesn't know whose wife she is, or whose daughter," Annie said. A citation could bring harm to the policeman and his family, and dog crap is not worth the risk.

I wondered how many other laws were not enforced for the same reason.

The Mafioso these days is not so often the gun-toting killer as he is the banker, the accountant, the parish priest, the lawyer, the architect, the cop, or the mayor—it could be anyone in a position of power, or anyone who owes a favor to someone higher up the food chain. Ordinary citizens never know whom they can trust, so they become suspicious and secretive. They stick to their family clans; I know two men who married their first cousins for just this reason. Blackmail and physical threats are still the Mafia's source of power. The harm doesn't always rifle down the barrel of a gun but hits its target just as surely through financial or emotional ruin. Now the Mafia kills slowly with asthma, ulcers, and nervous exhaustion.

I saw the effects of corruption everywhere I looked: the stolen sheep; the suspicious fire; the fixed lottery; the incompetent professor, hired as a favor; the "leaky" municipal water pipes; the ugly, illegal buildings encroaching on the Greek ruins in Agrigento's Valley of the Temples; right down to the dog dirt on city sidewalks. They call the Mafia *La Piovra*, "the octopus," because its tentacles reach into every aspect of daily life, and when one arm is cut off, another grows in its place. Some things haven't changed in centuries.

The day before Easter in 1986, my friend Piero, the fisherman, set his gill net in Mondello Bay. Easter morning his nets were gone, a mile of *tre maglie*, a three-ply net he had made himself, stolen right out of the water. Piero was visibly shaken; stealing his nets was like cutting off his hands. He couldn't work.

"Did you call the police?" I asked.

"The police are useless," he said. "I'm going to call a friend."

"What friend?"

He traced a line down his cheek with his thumbnail. A scarface type. Probably the one who controlled the territory.

The historian Denis Mack Smith wrote in *A History of Sicily: Medieval Sicily 800–1713* that by 1866, owing to lack of faith in changing governments, "Every Sicilian habitually disregarded official channels. His first recourse if he needed help was to kinsmen; but, in dealing with the threatening world of non-kin, he needed friends or 'friends of friends' whose patronage and system of contacts would help advance his family's fortune. These friends were people whose assistance he could claim in virtue of future allegiance, or else through some past service by himself or a relative."

Once, twenty years before, a Mafioso had asked Piero and a friend, two fishermen, to go out in their boats in the middle of the night to pick up floating boxes of black market Marlboros that were to be thrown off a passing ship and must be retrieved. Piero complied the one time he was asked, and the favor was not forgotten. Now Piero's Mafioso "friend" thought he might know of someone in nearby Vergine Maria who might know something about his stolen nets. The next day I answered the phone and took a message for Piero.

"It is possible," was all the man said. But the nets were never found, so Piero spent his summer nights sewing new ones in front of the television set.

❧   ❧   ❧

In December 1999 I was at a house party in Catania. The group was mostly twenty-somethings, young professionals. Alberto was a lawyer in the state attorney's office. "On Etna a priest will be tried for tying women up and raping them," he said.

"How was he finally found out?" I asked.

"Two people came forward only when he started taking their paychecks, or the greater part of them. It should come to trial in April."

"Good, then I can read about it in the papers," I said.

"The local papers won't publish anything about it because of their tight links with the Church. The same person owns both *La Sicilia* and *Il Giornale di Sicilia*." He implied that the Church and the newspapers do favors for each other. "The Church has all the power because it has all the money and all the votes. The Church is Sicily's only channel to power, so nobody wants to denounce it."

Denis Mack Smith wrote that, in 1876, "Sicilians might pretend that the mafia did not exist, and Sicilian newspapers kept astonishingly silent about it, yet in fact it crippled agriculture and industry."

The following May, while writing this book in Vermont, I found an on-line Milan newspaper that reported that Padre

Armando DiStefano, sixty-three, the parish priest of Mascalucia, an Etna village ten miles from Catania, had been accused of sexual violence, rape, and usury. He admitted lending the money to a habitual gambler but denied having charged him up to 144 percent interest. As for the rape, he said that two young mothers and a female student had "teased" him until he gave in. His alleged victims said the priest had turned the Bishop's Room, a parochial meeting room, into an illicit den of sex. When the women reminded him of his vow of celibacy, Padre DiStefano reportedly said that celibacy was the Church's decision, but that "God was surely against it."

When one woman had had enough, she said, Padre Armando threatened to tell her husband, then to rape her and her daughters. She said he subsequently tied her up and did rape her. Two of his older parishioners told the reporter they thought the priest was blameless and held him in high esteem. "He is a *gallantuomo*"—a gentleman—"and always at one's service."

Alberto, the lawyer who had alerted me to the case, said that as a conscientious objector, he had done two years of alternative civil service in an orphanage for encephalitic children. "Most of them are the children of prostitutes and their fathers are in jail," he said. The state money meant to clothe them went instead into administrators' pockets, he said, while the children wore used clothes. Staffers were sodomizing the children, Alberto said, but no one, not even Alberto, would report what they knew. Whistle blowers would lose their jobs, and work is so scarce that job openings were reported as news items in a column in *Il Giornale di Sicilia*, "Il Posto Che C'È"—"An Available Position."

Although Alberto had a volunteer job, he told me that if he had been the only witness, he would have lost the inevitable libel suit and would have paid enormous damages.

❦ ❦ ❦

In winter, western Sicily's foothills become rolling green mounds smelling of damp dirt and spring onions. One day, driving near Locati with Antonietta and Rosaria Riccobene, the twin sisters who were pharmacists, we came upon a farmer on a mare followed by a spindly-legged foal. He recognized the sisters' car and flagged us down. I got out and took pictures of the mare's bridle—scraps of leather tied together with bailing twine—and the homemade wooden saddle covered with burlap sacks. The foal nursed while the farmer showed the sisters the raw wounds on his mare's flank. He'd been dousing them with urine but they would not heal. The sisters—pharmacists, not veterinarians—advised him to stop the urine treatment and promised to make up a pomade for the mare. They had stayed in Locati for nine and a half years because they were brave, compassionate women and the agrarian people who live here had endeared themselves to them. In passing, the farmer said, "They robbed more of my sheep."

In the 1840's the most common crime in Sicily was the stealing of animals. According to Denis Mack Smith, the threat of cattle rustling then was used to extort protection money from landowners, and to make them employ criminals as guards on their estates. Sometimes whole herds disappeared overnight. One Italian-American friend said that when this happened to her grandfather's flock of sheep he immediately moved his family to America.

"It was impossible to control crime of this nature and on this scale," Smith wrote of the nineteenth-century Mafia. The police were corrupt. "Two or three times a year a company of troops would arrive in each village and round up a token number of malefactors, but this would be followed by another few months of complete impunity."

"Did you file a complaint?" Rosaria asked the farmer. She was one for using the laws, believing they would work if unhampered. He had reported the theft to the marshal, but the marshal had done nothing.

On the way back to Locati we figured out how much a dressed sheep would weigh and how much the meat was worth to the farmer. It came to about two hundred dollars, a huge loss.

"If the marshal does nothing, why doesn't he go to the marshal's superior?" I asked.

"His superior is scared too," Rosaria said. "The Mafiosi do what they want."

ê ê ê

Martina was one of the poorest people I had met in Sicily, a soft-spoken woman in her early thirties, the mother of a teenage girl. Her husband, Carlo, was out of work. They lived at the bottom of anyone's hierarchy in subsidized housing in

Locati, a village of red-orange tile rooftops nestled in a soft green valley rimmed by limestone cliffs and mountaintops. Their daughter slept on a cot in her parents' bedroom, the only bedroom in the house. Their bathroom had a sink and toilet but no shower or tub. They kept a Coke bottle filled with spring water in the refrigerator. Carlo climbed a mountain to reach the spring.

Wild things were free and Martina knew all the wild things that could serve: *sulla,* the peppery clover you could pick by the side of the road (peel the skin and eat the pith); pine nuts for making pesto; the succulent plant whose dried stalks can be fashioned into lightweight stools; the snails that can be eaten; the broken agave leaf, which oozes a liquid Martina's mother once used as laundry detergent when she used to wash clothes at the stream.

One morning Martina and Carlo invited me to spend the afternoon with them on a trip to Alimena, the next town over, where Carlo was born. I met them at their home—three rooms on two floors in an ancient apartment building on a hill in the heart of Locati. Carlo was mild-mannered and gaunt, with straight jet-black hair and high cheekbones. We climbed into his faded gray Fiat, all scratched and dented, and drove twenty minutes in intermittent downpours. The gray outskirts of Alimena were classic bleak, like a New Jersey wasteland, and gave me the same sinking feeling. Yet a sign welcomed us in English, German, and French.

"Are there tourists?" I asked, incredulous, from the backseat.

"In summer, yes. The children of emigrants," Carlo said. The old people who had remained welcomed their grandchildren back from Switzerland, Germany, Great Britain, and Australia, where there were jobs. "Those born abroad don't speak Italian anymore," he said. "Once they were all farmers. Do you know how many mules there were here once? The streets were full of shit."

Carlo drove us to the Church of Sant'Alfonso, high on a hill. The church was falling apart. He tried the door but it was locked. The town's patron saint was inside. "Alfonso," Carlo said. "We used to take him out during droughts."

"And then what happened?"

"Then it rained."

It was getting late. Martina had to prepare dinner and tend to the house. On the way back to Locati, the *carabinieri* stopped us. A cop in a Nazi-like uniform, with expensive sunglasses, glossy knee-high black boots, and a brimmed hat heavy with gilded vegetation came up to Carlo's window.

"*Documenti.*" He opened his hand. Carlo gave him his identification card, license, registration, and proof of insurance. The cop took Carlo to his patrol car parked in the intersection while Martina and I waited for fifteen minutes. Nothing happened.

"Why did they stop us?"

"Maybe they are looking for someone," Martina said. "Something must have happened."

Random traffic stops can turn up Mafiosi on the run. Carlo came back to report he was stopped for not wearing his seat belt. He went back to the officer. I started to watch the passing traffic; people in bigger, shinier cars sped by without seat belts. I was getting angry. *They stopped him because this car is old and shabby,* I thought. *He is obviously not rich and has no friends in high places. He is easy prey.* I was about to open the door and give them a piece of my mind when Martina grabbed my coat sleeve.

"They're always right," she said. "You can't argue. They stop the poor people. Not the ones who sell drugs, because they take a cut." It would hurt business.

Carlo finally came back. I asked what the fine was.

"A hundred thousand lire," he said, about 50 dollars. Their welfare check is only about $150 per month. I was mortified that our outing had ended like this.

Half a mile past the checkpoint, Carlo unlatched his seat belt and drove down the stripe in the middle of the road. It was the puerile, futile rebellion of a powerless man against the system.

Martina chatted on. She had seen an American film on Italian television. "It was about slaves in America. They beat them. They raped them. One white man asked a Negro lady for a glass of water. She gave it to him, then spat in it." Martina laughed. "This I liked."

Carlo kept his mouth shut. He'd already said the only thing he could say, and he said it without words. I saw it when I got out of the car in Locati, the faded sticker he had placed in the rear window years before, of a hand giving the finger to the world.

21

CASTIGLIONE DI SICILIA

જ્જ્જ

THE TOWN OF CASTIGLIONE, the "castle of the lion," was built
on a rock that dominates the Alcàntara valley on the northeast
slope of Mount Etna on the far eastern side of the island. In 730
B.C. the Greeks built a lookout tower on the great sandstone
rock to defend what was then the only road from the Ionian Sea
to the interior. In 496 B.C., exiles from Naxos, Sicily's first
Greek settlement, on the eastern coast, built a new city here.
Dionysius, tyrant of Syracuse, later destroyed it. The Romans
came and built bridges. The Arabs who followed them called
the valley Alcàntara, "river of many bridges." They revolution-
ized irrigation and even bred crocodiles in the Alcàntara River.
In the Middle Ages, Castiglione grew rich selling hazelnuts and
flax. Now, only a thousand people are left, mostly the old. The
town seal is embossed on white wastebaskets all over the village: two lions at rest flanking a stone tower topped by a crown.
The tower still stands at Castiglione's highest point, but its
round walls are missing many stones.

In the 1950's there was a hospital and two train stations here. The hospital is now closed, cobwebs bar doctors' doorways in the converted palaces of the aristocracy, and the only public transport is a bus. I'd been here before on day trips from Linguaglossa, but now I wanted to find a room with a family and stay a few days. Castiglione sits at the top of a lone mountain rising out of a hidden valley. You turn a corner and come upon it all at once—the tan houses stacked on the brown cliff looked like a Neapolitan crèche. At the foot of the cliff, sheep grazed knee-deep in winter grass. We zigzagged down into the valley and up again into Castiglione, melancholy in the rain.

Under the broken ramparts of the Greek fort the cliff face was burnt sienna. Brown lichen spread on the village's black walls; the lava glistened. Beads of rain dropped from the black vines of beaten iron curling above the plank door of a stone carriage shed. The lava-stone lintels were carved with grapes, fearsome masks, and stylized wild roses. Higher up in town, white limestone rimmed an oval porthole in a lava wall and creeping vines grew through it. The portal framed the deep valley and descending orange rooftops of the newer houses on the edge of town. Overhead, drooling gargoyles upheld some balconies. Palm trees bent before the snow-capped volcano.

The bus stopped in Piazza Sammartino. Twenty pensioners in navy-blue pea coats and scarves wound twice round their necks eyed me as I walked to the Trefilletti Bar and ordered a cup of hot tea. The aged woman at the counter couldn't manage the steam machine so I switched my order to an amaretto. She poured me four fingers and told me of a woman around the corner who might have rooms. She wrote down the name but I didn't understand her directions. It takes a while to tune one's ear to the dialect of each new town. She pointed over my shoulder and said, "This boy will take you." I turned around. In the orange plastic chair under the orange plastic pay phone slouched a man who appeared to be in his late sixties, with bad hair, worse teeth, and ill-fitting clothes. "His name is Peppe." When he stood up the crotch of his pants hung around his knees. "He is an honest boy of this town whom you can trust," the old woman said. The man said nothing and never looked at me but led me dutifully two blocks to the door of Signora Cammulia. I rang, turned around, and old Peppe was gone.

A lady opened. "I'm looking for a room," I said.

"You have the face of a *paesana*, a countrywoman," she said. *My grandparents' gift to me*, I thought. She was sure she recognized me from somewhere. She showed me the apartment, five cold rooms, one of them with a broken door to the second-floor balcony. Too big and too drafty, and I'd be alone. I decided to look farther. Her daughter-in-law drove me to the town's upper piazza, where I stopped in another bar.

I thought I'd found a lost village, but hanging on the wall were autographed photos of Harvey Keitel, looking buff in a muscle T-shirt, standing behind the bar with the owner and his family. "He was here for a month making a film," the owner said. Castiglione had been scouted by Cinecittà as a setting for a film called *The Vipers*. The photo was signed in thick black marker in Italian: "To you, and the beautiful time we shared together. I hold it forever. Harvey Keitel."

I made Vincenzo Fallone's bar my base in this part of town. His wife filled me in on Our Lady of the Chain, whose statue is brought out of the church of the same name in procession only once every five years. The Madonna is covered in gold necklaces, watches, bracelets, and brooches. Once a man tried to steal the gold and jewels but stuck to the statue until the next morning, she said. The priest called the cops but they couldn't budge the thief. When Mass was over the Virgin finally released him to the *carabinieri*. Vincenzo introduced me to a man who knew the thief personally. Another pensioner walked me to the Church of Our Lady of the Chain. It was locked, but he got the key from the lady who cleans it. The interior was all heavenly white and gold, freshly painted, with a new organ and chandeliers.

I couldn't find a room but left my name with Vincenzo, who said he'd make a few calls for me. I left to walk my favorite path, which started at Fallone's door. The sweetest street in Castiglione was a horseshoe-shaped footpath carved into the mountain behind town. Round dimpled green leaves bobbed from the cliff face on fine stems while the raindrops beat them silly. Near the summit, a thousand-year-old church grew from the same weathered brown stone, a broad monolith whose sinews gripped the ground.

Vincenzo found me a room, and after New Year's I came for a stay. My host, Salvatore Chìsari, sold his hand-made furniture (carved gilt swirls and red velvet) from a shop attached to his house. The store was never open because Salvatore was always tending his rabbits or olives, hazelnuts or kitchen garden, or was at one of his country places, tending vines, making wine, or cutting wood for the fireplace. I had my own room downstairs with two single beds, a pine armoire he'd made, a table, two chairs, and a panoramic view. A cold gray rain pelted the two glass doors that gave out onto an abrupt, deep valley. Directly below were the tops of Signore Chìsari's nearest fruit trees, then there was a quick drop-off to dots of sheep and the river far below. High up to the right was Motta Camastra, a clutch of white-cube houses clinging to a white cliff. Below and to the left were the lights of Francavilla di Sicilia.

Three red-hot bars of light glowed futilely from the electric heater on the cold tile floor. I turned my mattress warmer on "high" and listened to a dog howl all night in the beating rain and in the morning I heard the distant clanging of sheep bells.

Adriano, the Chìsaris' son, had eight more university exams to pass before he got his degree in architecture. In the meantime he was licensed to design and supervise construction of buildings no taller than two stories. Antonella, his thirty-three-year-old sister, was an abstract artist studying for a teacher's certificate. In the meantime she had a part-time job at the town office, "doing nothing," she said. I went to visit her office one day. She sat in an empty room, at an empty desk with no phone other than her own cell phone, no paper clutter, no assignment, but it had a nice window with colorful stained-glass panes. Her job was the fruit of a law that created "socially useful work," a government workfare program. She sat in the unheated office with her coat on and made her personal phone calls.

Antonella's mother, Graziella, was a housewife who in her spare time made cutwork sheets and curtains. Her handiwork boggled my mind. Each sheet could contain three thousand embroidered holes. She sold her work for a thousand lire per puncture and had so many customers willing to pay $1,500 for a set of fine sheets that she parceled out orders to her friends and took a commission.

The Dalmatian, Juri, completed the family. Like a lot of Sicilian males, he was handsome, boisterous, transgressive, pampered, and rude. They let him roam the streets and he always returned with cuts on his face and ears, but Antonella adored him. "He is so beautiful that people are jealous and want him dead. I am afraid someone will feed him a poison meatball." It wouldn't be the first time in Sicily.

There wasn't much to do in Castiglione in the winter rain. I stayed inside with my wool hat on and lingered long at the Chìsaris' table. Signore Chìsari told me jokes in Sicilian and when I didn't get them he tried to teach me his dialect. Antonella showed me her charcoal sketches—many dark visions of Etna. I photographed Graziella with sheets on her lap working in what light came through the balcony door. I read every word of *Gente*, my Italian *People* magazine. To get into the library I would have had to attend seven o'clock Mass and get the library keys from the priest. That never worked out. One day the Chìsaris took me to Motta Camastra, where the streets are so narrow that we had to back up to the edge of town when we met another car. So sometimes, just to get out of the house and stay dry, I went back to the Trefilletti Bar.

The owner was a blue-eyed redhead nicknamed Il Danese, "the Dane," for his coloring. He was neither handsome nor boisterous, just transgressive and rude. One afternoon, out of the blue, he got on his soapbox and announced, "I talked with the priest and he agreed with me that the cemetery is a field of lies." His ten-year-old son sat at a bar table doing his homework, trying to write a fable. His wife was wiping down the counter. Maybe it was the rain, or the short days, or maybe I'd stayed too long in this gloomy town, but he'd hit a deep nerve.

"What do you mean?" I asked.

"Gravestones say nice things when the dead person might have beaten his wife, or been a murderer."

I don't know why, but I started to cry. I thought, *My mother's gravestone has nothing on it but her name and two dates.* Tears dripped down both cheeks; it was absurd but I couldn't hold them back. His wife noticed and I hoped she'd say, "Let's change the subject," but instead she came to watch. They both seemed energized by my tears.

His wife said, "She's like me, too sensitive." Then the Dane dug in again. He thought I should get over it and gave me all his reasons why. He blew hot air and paused every so often to invite me to "reason" with him. (Read "argue.") I should have turned on my heels and walked out but I didn't want him to feel as though he'd won this silly showdown. When I did try to leave he had me first say goodbye to his son to regain my composure. He couldn't have his clients be seen leaving in tears.

22

"MY FLOWERS WERE OF STONE"

ॐ

IN CASTIGLIONE, I found a new bar, Il Presidente, in a side street that fed into Piazza Sammartino. Laura, the owner, was behind the counter. She pulled out a copy of an Italian travel magazine devoted entirely to Sicily and in particular to the towns on Etna's slopes. I flipped through the images of orange molten lava, mountain fireworks, rock climbers, and skiers. Castiglione was in there, too.

"The pictures are nice," she said, "but here's the reason I showed this to you." She opened to a picture of a man bent over a workbench. "This is my brother. He does stone inlay. Maybe he would talk to you." I scanned the article. The author complained about how hard it was to pin this man down, despite his three cell phone numbers. But Laura dialed the secret numbers, told her brother she had a journalist who wanted a word with him, and passed me the phone.

"Why are you here?" he asked.

"Because I love the stones," I said. I thought I might have to explain, but he set a date to meet me at Vincenzo Fallone's bar. He would take me to his workshop in the country, where we could talk while he worked.

The rain sluiced down the narrow streets for two more days but softened to a mist on the morning of the interview. I found him in front of the bar, smoking a Marlboro, looking as though he was waiting for somebody. He was forty-six, with close-cropped salt-and-pepper hair, a handsome face, high cheekbones, a model's bearing, and some missing teeth. He couldn't take me to his workshop because the rain had swollen the creek below his studio. He nodded at his fourteen-year-old beat-up red car. "She won't get through it," he said. So he took me to a pocket piazza nearby, near a church. He leaned against a stone balustrade as pigeons swooped over the tile rooftops below, and tapped out a cigarette. "So what exactly are you writing about?" he asked.

"The people I find in small Sicilian mountain towns."

For the next hour and a half, he told me his life story, but he asked me first to change his name to "Joe Fox." True or false, it was a hell of a story.

He was born poor, and the poor were considered stupid even if they were smart, he said, while the dimwitted sons of lawyers and pharmacists were considered intelligent only because they had money. His mother had died when he was ten—as had mine. "The child's play was over." I knew what he meant. At an early age he could see his life through the wrong end of the telescope. "If we watched a film, others laughed, but I was bored." He learned to amuse himself. He liked to draw, sit by streams, play with rocks. He carved shapes out of the softer ones. His mother told him on her deathbed that he should become an artist who worked with stone.

When he was fourteen his luck changed. Fate had made him handsome. All summer he and his friends prowled the beaches, hotels, and discos of Taormina. "With tourists, it was free love. With Sicilian girls, it was different." In the winter he went to school and worked for an artisan in marble. He told me he sold his first piece of marble sculpture to Tennessee Williams, who came to Castiglione in the summers with his friend, Riccardo. When Joe Fox was older, he went to Florence to study the art of inlay. The public universities rejected him because he had no one to put in a good word, and the private schools were too expensive. "Without connections, you can't make any headway," he said. So he went to work designing T-shirts and jeans for a cousin's clothing business in Venezuela to earn tuition for a private art school in Florence.

In Caracas, the rich daughter of an Italian-American businessman fell in love with him. She flew around on a private jet. "I entered into this absurdly rich world that all poor people, at least once, dream to live in," Joe Fox said. They were a couple for two or three years, but he wasn't sure whether he was in love with the girl or her money. Her family pressured him for a decision. "I have never been a slave to money, but the life was so golden. I went away to think about it. It was May." He flew to Miami to think, met a violinist on the beach, had sex with her, and realized he didn't miss the Venezuelan. He reflected for ten more days in New York at the Plaza Hotel, between shopping sprees and Broadway musicals. But one night he realized that money didn't fill the hole inside him, so he went back to Caracas and ended his relationship. One night friends invited him to a dinner.

The guest of honor was a strange old man who lived as a hermit in the Amazon jungle, a former diamond hunter turned scholar and student of jungle flora. Every so often he went to the police or to a journalist to say what he had found. Joe Fox sat next to him and asked him why he lived in the jungle.

"He never answered my question. All night he would not even say *sì* or *no*. Was he being rude? Was he crazy? At the end, I asked him to take me to the jungle."

The guest of honor shook his hand and said he'd expect Joe in fifteen days on the Island of the Orchids.

"Where is it?" Joe asked.

The hermit told him that was his own damn problem. "If you get there, fine. If not, nothing."

Joe made it to the Island of the Orchids with the help of a family of *indios* and their boat. Near dusk the hermit arrived in a leaky canoe and took Joe to his hut at an encampment.

"So, from this moment, you must know that all the animals who live here know that you have arrived," the hermit said. Joe was afraid of snakes, and here they were all poisonous. He set his hammock up high, and his shoes, too, so scorpions would not crawl into them. He'd go to sleep terrorized. The next day he'd say "Good morning" to the hermit, but the hermit never responded. This went on for more than a week. On the tenth day that Joe said "Good morning" the hermit left and came back at noon with fruits, fish, and roots, and finally spoke.

"Why do you always say 'Good morning'? What does it mean? Here you are not in the office. I'm alive, you're alive, and the day is beautiful. What the hell does it mean, 'Good morning'?" the hermit said.

Joe asked why he had been invited to the island, and the hermit said it was because Joe was the only one at that dinner who didn't ask him where the diamonds were. "I looked for diamonds but it was the one inside I found," the hermit said. He had been in the jungle forty years now studying plants. They made a truce, and Joe decided to stay six weeks. He stopped greeting the hermit in the morning.

One day the hermit took Joe on a day-long hike up a mountain to where a river cut through the center of a bare rock as wide as a soccer field, surrounded by thick jungle. Joe was moved by the sight. "This rock was at the center of God's thoughts," he said. He had brought his Walkman; he plugged in Vivaldi's "Four Seasons" and sat by the cascading river, in the center of the rock in the sunlight, in an ecstasy. "It was the unrepeatable center of my existence," he said. "Maybe even my body was gone." The transcendent experience made him cry for the beauty of simple things. "I was free and uncontrollable. The door to my life was opened," he said. When Joe came back to earth, the hermit said to him, "You've been here almost two months, in the realm of plants and flowers. As soon as you find a rock, you rise above. You don't climb trees, you sleep on rocks. Why?"

"When he finished the question, I understood," Joe Fox said. "My flowers were of stone. I left."

After a trip to Ayers Rock in Australia (just to be sure) and a week of sex with a troubled American psychiatrist on Dunc Island, a resort off the Australian coast, he went to school in Florence to finally study stone inlay, then returned to Castiglione to ply his trade. They were hard times with no commissions. Friends lent him money to eat and to buy stone. Now, after years of struggle, his stone inlay of Castiglione's medieval seal hangs in the town office, and his works sell for thousands of dollars.

ॐ ॐ ॐ

Days later Joe Fox drove me to his studio, a hazelnut storage shed behind an orchard at the foot of a hill a mile from town. The flooded brook came up to his hubcaps.

"When I was a kid I would cut school and sit by this stream all day," he said. "It fascinated me, and still does—the history rolling by, coming from a spring and going to the ocean, rolling over rocks and sand, pulverizing stone, wearing things down, changing them, sustaining them, paying no attention to us." He said he always got a beating when he got home, "but it was worth it." Once past the gate he parked the car and we walked up a footpath that wound through the bare hazelnut trees.

He asked me to wait at a distance while he put his dog, Gianluca Barberini Odelscalchi, in his pen. He looked to be part Airedale, part German shepherd, and was named after a noble Roman who had become pope. "He is a bastard, a mix of all the races that came to Sicily."

The shed was one square room. Light entered from two windows and the open door. A sloping roof of plastered cane stalks rested on wooden beams. The giant oval leaves of an old prickly pear blocked Joe's view of his small vineyard. Chains of dried red peppers and garlic hung on the wall. One bare light bulb dangled from a wire. Etna filled the other window. The snow had descended to its very lower slopes and the sun had glazed it iceberg white, set in a stone-blue sky.

A pile of semiprecious stones ground flat and thin as crackers lay in the sunlight on the work table, their frosted colors full of promise: matte turquoise, lapis lazuli, honey-colored tiger's-eye, white opal, creamy agate, and jungle-green malachite. He cut shapes of out these. To avoid being fractured or chipped, each crystal wafer needed its own touch when he cut them, into long-tailed parrots, hummingbirds, and tropical flowers. The stones interlocked like a jigsaw puzzle in a marble slab chiseled to hold them. Later he would polish the stone painting. I sat in his doorway and looked at Etna while he chinked away, the calming music of a craftsman absorbed in his work.

The Woman in the Mask was a work in progress. She was haunting in a feline mask, symbol of the gods' unpredictable cruelty, with a diamond-shaped white opal in the center of her forehead. He had cut shimmering yellow and brown tiger's-eye for her cat eyes, which had no pupils. She was unpolished, so he splashed her face with water to make her colors come up. Her dead eyes followed me; her directionless gaze encompassed all.

"Stones don't die," he said. He picked up a chunk of lapis lazuli and walked over to the window with it and held the stone close to his eyes. "Now that I have had everything, I dream of this death: While I look through that blue, inside that blue, to go back to eternity. All I want now is a death worthy of the stones."

23

CASTELLO ROMEO

❧

JOE FOX TOOK ME to meet some friends one night at Castello Romeo, a restaurant in an eighteenth-century country villa on the road to Randazzo. The sky was black, the stars were faint, and the moon cast a pearly sheen on the white volcano. Joe's friend and his wife picked us up in a Mercedes sedan and we drove under a stone arch up a tree-lined lane to a small mansion stuccoed smoky pink. We parked behind it, near a long-disused stable and an overgrown "English" garden. The restaurant was in a long hall in a separate wing. Painted murals covered the walls. We sat near the kitchen with our hosts, the owner, Signore Scrivano, and his wife. He owned this place and the Hotel Scrivano, the only hotel in nearby Randazzo. A fire blazed in a stone hearth at the other end of the room. The restaurant was filling with Rotarians who'd come for a monthly dinner meeting. Their wives milled around at the fireplace, under the television set on the mantel.

While the men pontificated on how best to serve boiled calf's head—hot or cold?—and the women at the table discussed their difficulties with curtains, I warmed myself at the fireplace and watched the lottery drawing on TV. In Italy, this is no quick break between commercials with a hostess reading numbers off whiffle balls. This is a half-hour extravaganza of transparency, to prove nothing crooked is going on, with a handsome blue-eyed host, sequined babes, a band, and a chorus line.

The drawing goes like this: A woman places a black mask on the face of an eight-year-old boy—an innocent still incapable of sin; he'll make his first confession when he turns nine—and tightens two drawstrings to snug it in place. The boy raises his right hand to show that it is empty. Nearby a man churns a bingo basket full of identical white plastic balls and has the boy withdraw one. A woman in a business suit presses a fishbowl under his hand; he drops it in and she passes the bowl to a man at a table who removes the sphere, unscrews its two halves, holds up the numbered slip of paper it contains, and passes that to a woman seated beside him. She records the number in a ledger, then smoothes the paper out for the camera and the studio audience to see. "First drawing, number sixty!" she announces. A curvy blonde in a blue Barbie gown repeats, "First drawing, number sixty!" The man at the table rings a little hand bell, and the tender scene is repeated five more times. The whole show lasts twenty minutes. Later I learned there'd been a scandal years earlier: Crooks froze the balls they wanted chosen just before the show and told the boy always to pick the coldest one. I went back to the table.

"It's all true!" Scrivano said. He was telling a story about his father. "You can look it up in the *Giornale di Sicilia*."

His father was an eighty-year-old widower with a fifty-year-old girlfriend who had two grown children. He showered this girlfriend with clothes, jewelry, and money. "He wanted her to move in with him. But she said she had problems with her children, so she would spend three nights a week with my father, then two nights with her children, then again two nights with him. So he'd have her company five nights a week. That is, if he paid her." Scrivano shrugged. "He was in love with her. Finally he realized she was a *puttana*"—a woman who traded sex for money. "He took a kitchen knife and stabbed her in the heart. Split her heart in two." She had to have open-heart surgery, but she survived, Scrivano said.

Meanwhile, his father took off for Floresta, the highest village in Sicily, near Mount Etna, and hid out in a shepherd's hut. "When shepherds came in, he played dead. They left and went to the *carabinieri* at Santa Domenica Vittoria to report the dead body. Of course, my father left the hut as soon as the shepherds were gone. He stopped a logging truck that took him back to Randazzo. I hid him in the Scrivano Hotel and got him to take a shower. He couldn't be an eighty-year-old man on the lam."

Scrivano convinced his father to make a deal with the police: He would give himself up at the barracks without a scene in exchange for no publicity. The *carabinieri* double-crossed him and called the journalists. They were waiting downstairs in the lobby while Scrivano snuck his father out the back exit. At the barracks, police handcuffed him. "The handcuffs were the kind with the thorn in the middle. This was too much. My father wanted to know only whether he had killed that *puttana*."

His father raised pedigreed livestock, top quality, and was proud of his herd. "He gave free meat to the poor. Everybody loved him," Scrivano said. His father was just a hair from being an assassin, "but he was a good man, and brave."

"When the judge asked him if he had meant to kill that woman, he stood up and faked being blind." His crooked doctor had certified him as legally blind and had been taking a percentage of his disability check, but he could see as well as anyone. "My father said, 'No, Judge. I loved that woman. I dressed her well. I just took a butter knife and waved it. It was an accident.' "

The woman survived her heart surgery. Scrivano and his brothers went to her and offered her "enough money to buy two houses" if she would drop charges. "We all had a good laugh when we went to see her. Even the *puttana* laughed."

Scrivano's father died at eighty-five after being hit by a car that careened onto the sidewalk at a street market, but didn't kill him right away. When his time did come, Scrivano's wife said, "he knew," and he wanted to die dapper. One day he took her shopping. "We were to buy him a fantastic suit, new clothes, and new underwear," she said. He had her lock these in a chest. Then he picked out his casket. "He told me to buy the shoes later because his feet might swell when he was dead." He warned her not to buy hard leather shoes but soft ones instead. "He always bought two-hundred-thousand-lire shoes. You know what he did with those shoes? He put them on, then took a sharp knife and cut a hole for his bunion."

He left three million lire in a cup on a high shelf in the kitchen. "No one but me knew about it," his daughter-in-law said. When he died, and she was done paying the funeral expenses (he said flowers were fine but not necessary) she had spent 2,900,000 lire. His other daughter-in-law, whom he hated because she had treated his first wife badly when she was sick, wanted 100,000 lire to pay for calls the old man had made from her phone. "How did he know exactly how much to leave to cover his expenses?" she asked. "When he died, all of Randazzo was at his funeral, because he was a good man."

I thought to myself, *The Dane was right. The cemetery is a field of lies.*

24

GRIM REAPER

ༀ

Few modern Western cultures go to such extremes as Sicilians in their ritualization of death.

Once I was visiting my friend Rosa on the island of Favignana, off the coast of Tràpani. Every spring on her island men chase giant bluefin tuna through their trap's flowered portal into a chamber of death, and sing while they pull up their net, songs so old they don't know what some words mean. Rosa is the cemetery custodian, and now she was busy removing dead flowers from the cone-shaped vases affixed to tombstones. While I waited for her to finish, I pulled my Walkman from my daypack and found a seat with a view of a powder-blue bay and listened to Arvo Pärt's *Litany*. Over the music I heard a woman screaming. Following her cries, I ran through the mausoleum alleys to where she stood next to an open grave. She was wailing. Her knees buckled, and two men in suits kept her from falling in. Rosa took my elbow and led me away quietly. The woman was performing the rites that her townspeople expected of her. "She is exaggerating," Rosa said. "But it was her father who died."

In Gibellina, I heard, one can still hire professional mourners to perform this graveside ritual. The old hill town was the epicenter of the 1968 earthquake that destroyed my relatives' homes in nearby Santa Margherita. Hundreds died when the walls of their houses fell upon them. Some years later, an artist from northern Italy, Alberto Burri, covered the rubble in a cement shroud that he plastered smooth and white. *Gibellina Entombed* was said to be the world's largest sculpture. Burri's shroud followed the contours of the village like a sheet draped over a corpse. When I visited in 1992 I linked arms with a friend and walked through what used to be streets. Nothing came higher than my chest. Here and there the sheet would rise where a fountain had been, or where a house or a courtyard wall had once stood. Those whose bodies could not be found or removed were under there still. The sheet went on for acres, uphill and surreal.

୬ ୬ ୬

I came to Lìpari, one of the volcanic Aeolian Islands, in the Tyrrhenian Sea off the north coast of Messina province, to celebrate the death and birth of a year, decade, century, and millennium with Carmelo Bua and his family and twenty-five of their friends in an inn owned by the Buas, La Casa del Vescovo, "the bishop's house." It had been the residence of Fra Benedetto Re, the late bishop of Lìpari, a lame man who dragged his foot. When Fra Re died, in the nineteen-sixties, he bequeathed his house to the diocese, which leased it to my friends, who ran it as a *pensione* in the summer. Sometimes people who sleep in the house hear a footstep followed by a sound like a sack being dragged across the floor.

Lìpari and its sister islands in the Tyrrhenian Sea— Panarea, Salina, Vulcano, Alicudi, Filicudi, and Stròmboli— are the home of Aeolus, the Greek god of the wind (they are also called the Lìpari Islands). In the summer Aeolus sends soft breezes for the supermodels and Hollywood stars who island-hop from Lìpari to Panarea, blessing restaurants and discos with their crowd-drawing presence. But now it was winter, it was raining, and the Casa del Vescovo was gloomy without heat.

As guests arrived from the ferry landing they propped their cell phones on a bookshelf and took off their coats, but I wore mine inside. There was no television or radio, because Carmelo would allow neither. An engineer in a noisy city, he came here to cleanse and recharge. We played cards and board games and listened to stories.

Carmelo's youngest daughter said she once heard a choir of angels in her room, and Fra Re had appeared in her dreams. "Someone bangs on the water tank at night," Carmelo said. "Someone rattles the windows." They had requested a priest in Patti to say a Mass for the liberation of Fra Re's soul, and they were waiting to see what would happen.

At midnight we toasted with spumante and ate lentils for luck. The kids set off fireworks, the church bell rang, and the cell phones beeped and shrilled. We stepped out onto the porch to watch the coastal lights for signs of a Y2K blackout, some watching with hope, some with fear, but nothing happened. I kept my coat on in bed. I lay between the damp sheets with a bottle of hot tap water and hoped Naomi Campbell and Tom Cruise were someplace warm and dry.

The next morning the wind god sent hail. I stood on the porch and watched the cold glass stones pile up at my feet. The bishop's house was on a hillside overlooking the Greek citadel and the sea behind it. The sun punched a hole in the clouds and rays played on choppy gray waves. To my right, three volcanoes lined up in a row: Monte Chirica, Lìpari's own; Monte Aria on Vulcano; and snow-covered Etna.

Carmelo's friend the undertaker, Bartulo Russo, stopped in on New Year's morning for an espresso corrected by amaretto.

Of the ten thousand inhabitants of the Aeolian Islands, ninety to ninety-five die every year, he said, and he and his brothers take care of them all. When a person dies anywhere in the archipelago, islanders call the Russos. They alert the priest, go to the typesetters, paste up the death notices, and have the grave dug. The brothers wash the body in the dead person's home, dress it, place it in a casket, and provide the little electric lamps that flicker at the deceased's head and feet. They do not embalm. In summer they place a border of flowers around the body to mask unpleasant odors, and cover the open coffin with a mosquito net to keep the flies at bay.

By law, the body must lie in an open casket at the cemetery in a room equipped with a bell for twenty-four hours before interment, so in the case of coma or apparent death, "the presumed cadaver can wake up and give the alarm," he said.

Recently the Lìpari cemetery was getting too crowded, so they started the common practice of exhuming the long-dead and putting their bones in boxes to make room for new arrivals. "I am one of the firms authorized to do such work," Russo said.

I wondered how he came to this profession.

"It was born as a joke among three brothers," he said. They never did quit their day jobs. One brother was a commercial accountant, one did landscaping, and one sold farm equipment. No school or degree is necessary to become an undertaker, just a license to operate as businessmen or artisans, Russo said. The brothers learned to tend the dead by watching their elders, who used to do it for members of their own families.

Once they found half a man in the sea, with mussels attached to his scuba suit. One night they recovered another from the sea near the island of Stròmboli, who was also missing half his body. He was from Catania, Russo said, and had fallen into the sea, or had been pushed, from a ship that sailed between Naples and Palermo. One night at 2 A.M. they were called to fish a whole corpse, terribly bloated, out of the sea. "We put on our masks and rubber gloves for that one."

As undertakers on a volcanic island, they have had some special body retrievals. They have collected dead tourists from the crater of the still-active volcano on Stròmboli. "Maybe even an American. Germans, for sure." People often fell into the live crater, until island officials prohibited access without a licensed guide.

If a deceased tourist is Italian, the brothers accompany the body to its final destination. Foreigners get a lift to the Catania airport. They sent the remains of one woman who had fallen into the volcano back to Czechoslovakia, but her relatives didn't pay up for a year, so now survivors of deceased foreigners must pay Russo in advance. The average cost of an Aeolian funeral is three or four million lire, about two thousand dollars. That includes flowers, priest, casket, care of the corpse, printing, permits, affixing the posters, cemetery workers' fees, and transport in a dark-gray hearse. On Alicudi, the smallest island, which has no roads, the cemetery is the archipelago's highest. The casket must be carried uphill on the pallbearers' shoulders. "In the summer, it is hot work," Russo said.

৵৹   ৵৹   ৵৹

In a cool crypt below the Convento dei Cappuccini, the Capucin monastery in Palermo, hundreds of desiccated, centuries-old corpses dressed in their Sunday best lean drunkenly in wall niches, their faces frozen into ghoulish grins. The friar collecting coins in a silver tray at the entrance said the mummies originally numbered seven or eight thousand, but the bones of corpses that had crumbled had been moved to an ossuary. Several hundred can still be seen.

Postmortem display became fashionable in the eighteenth century. The powerful and rich, rather than disappearing beyond the grave, opted instead for a showy niche in the crypt. Most of the corpses still have eyeballs, fingernails, hair, skin, and teeth. The gentlemen wear tall hats, tailored suits, and good shoes, the ladies their gowns and tiaras. The bishop wears his miter and holds a staff; military men stand in uniform. The children have a hall of their own. The women who died virgins wear crowns and are kept locked behind bars. The dead monks, the oldest corpses here, wear their belted brown robes. One who died in 1699 wears the rope belt around his neck because his lower half has been replaced by a burlap bag stuffed with straw. One monk is just a skull; lovers have written their names in a heart on it. The most recent corpse admitted, in the 1920's, was the child Rosalia, a young girl with smooth cheeks and a ribbon in her long, blond ringlets. She looks like a doll in a glass coffin.

I asked the friar at the door what had to be done to keep so many dead people in shape. From time to time, he said, the brothers have changed the clothes of certain male corpses, but they never lay hands on the women. "Other than that," he said, "we just dust."

25

FOOD IS THE FONT OF LOVE

SICILIANS EAT FROM THEIR OWN SEA AND SOIL, so the fish and produce on their tables change with the seasons. Vendors display food like art. The fishmonger's rainbow *viole* are jewels set in shaved ice, so pretty it seems a shame to char them in a frying pan. A greengrocer places one purple eggplant next to four perfect red peppers on an overturned crate outside her store. Garlic vendors wear stoles made of the papery entwined bulbs. Oranges and pears come wrapped in gold-leafed red tissue paper. In August in Palermo, men build pyramids of watermelons stacked like green cannonballs on street corners. In winter in Palermo's souklike Vucciria market, the bulk-tomato-paste man sculpts a huge heart from the stiff pulp and leaves his knife plunged into the blood-red mass. All this food ends up on the kitchen table, the heart of every home.

A family consists of the faces at that table, the ones Mamma sustains with her tomato sauce, the boiling pot and the promise of pasta. Any meal is to a Sicilian what a madeleine was for Proust, a gateway to reverie.

When I lived with Piero and his fishermen friends in Mondello, on winter nights we'd walk around the corner to visit Zia Ciccina in Via Delfini, so named because when the women who lived there chattered they sounded like so many dolphins. We wedged in elbow to elbow around Zia Ciccina's upstairs kitchen table with her husband, their two bachelor sons, their married daughter, her two boys, and Signora Angelina, her daughter's mother-in-law. They were playing *scopa*; it was Zia Ciccina's deal, and she was winning.

"How do you win this game?" I asked Ciccina.

"You cheat," Signora Angelina said.

They shouted, swore in Sicilian, laughed, smoked Dianas, and slammed cards on the table. The kids ran in and out of the room in their pajamas, just bathed and smelling of soap. A hundred baby artichokes boiled away in a pot. The steam fogged the windows and made the tiny room even closer. Zia Ciccina drained the bite-sized chokes, drizzled them with olive oil, and sprinkled them with sea salt and we ate them like peanuts from a common bowl.

Even a sandwich on the lonely road brings comfort. On Etna, at the crossroads in Linguaglossa, there used to be a dark *bottega* that smelled of salami and strawberries. Rosario Cavallaro, the owner, once invented a *panino*, a little sandwich, just for me: pecorino cheese, pickled peppers, capers, and fresh tomato on fragrant yellow bread, chewy as steak and smeared with olive oil. He wouldn't let me pay. I wrapped the sandwich in two napkins but its fragrance seeped through my daypack. All morning while I took pictures of stone walls, that essence followed me like a benevolent spirit. Later, on the train, I wrote an ode to my lunch and mailed the poem to Rosario.

ॐ ॐ ॐ

Eleonora Consoli cracked an egg into a glass bowl of chopped veal, and *via!* she plunged in her hands. The orange yolk streaked through the pink meat. She was preparing an "arrosto," Sicilian stuffed cutlets.

"The hands are a cook's gold," she told her class of three women from nearby Trecastagni and San Giovanni Lo Punto. We were in her three-hundred-year-old house in Viagrande, a small town on Etna's southern flank, named for the "great road" built in the 1920's to take tourists up to the craters.

Her kitchen floor was tiled with terra-cotta squares. Copper pots hung from a beam overhead. A framed homage from Eleonora's seven-year-old granddaughter hung at the kitchen entrance as a blessing on the room. She had drawn hearts and printed in her child's hand: "Little grandmother, you are too good and I love you too much you are the most beautiful grandmother in the world you are the best cook and you love me right? Answer here. Yes. No. *Viva Nonna!*"

Eleonora Consoli is the author of *La Cucina del Sole* (*Cuisine of the Sun*), a 1986 book honoring Sicilian cooking from the time before the *monzù*. These were chefs who, in the nineteenth century, were sent by Sicilian nobles to be trained in French courts (the word actually is the French *monsieur*, modified to fit the Sicilian tongue). The *monzù* introduced, among other things, butter and cream sauces to Sicilian cooking. Eleonora, now sixty-five, sought recipes that predated the *monzù*, and gathered them from people in up-country towns, where she was usually welcomed into their kitchens and lives. Her book helped revive interest and pride in local ingredients and regional cooking.

She added chopped walnuts and parsley to the veal and wrapped the mixture in triangular patches of pounded turkey cutlets. She poked holes in these and inserted tiny cubes of ham, then tied each packet up with string, ready for the frying pan. She sliced onions into a skillet and the women gathered at the stove. The stuffed turkey cutlets slowly turned golden. Eleonora added cloves and a little water, then covered the pot, and lit a cigarette. After a while, she cocked an ear to the sizzle. "It's frying!" The sound filled her with joy. "The meat is finished when it sounds like this."

Next on the menu were *arancini*, "little oranges," fried rice balls the size of oranges, in two shapes. The round ones contain red sauce with meat. The pyramids contain a mixture of tuma cheese, peas, and bits of ham. The Arabs brought rice to Sicily, she said, where it was an important crop in the eighteenth and nineteenth centuries. "Wet your hands before touching it." Her students packed boiled white rice between their palms; each one came out the shape of the hands that made it. Eleonora dunked the *arancini* in flour, egg, breadcrumbs, salt, pepper, and parsley before deep-frying them.

Hands on hips, she looked at a sizzling string of sausage. "Too bad we didn't make potatoes." She looked at me. "Do you like fried potatoes?" Eleonora's assistant ran to get some and we smiled to ourselves as we peeled and sliced.

Then she cut up a cauliflower for her "suffocated cauliflower" casserole. The Etna variety of cauliflower is violet-colored, while Palermo cauliflowers are purplish. Eleonora once made a centerpiece from a local cauliflower with violet orchid sprigs stuck into it. In a deep pot she layered cauliflower slices with olive oil, cheese, onions, olives, green peppers, and sardines, then added a dash of wine and glugs of olive oil. This she covered with a lid that was too small and weighted it with a rock to press it down. She set it on a burner to cook. When dinner was ready, we feasted.

The dining-room floor was covered with a red Turkish rug. A cast-iron and glass Venetian chandelier hung over the table. A wraparound mural surrounded us with the countryside of Eleonora's childhood summers, the soft colors of thirsty dirt in the high plains of Caltanisetta, in the island's interior. "Before you get to Enna, the country is all like this," she said. The wine was homemade, the gift of her gardener. The talk at table was of food.

"Food is the font of love," Eleonora said. The love-food relationship begins when a mother suckles her child. "This first relationship—the strongest bond—is expressed through food and nurture," she said. When friends and family feast, it is always an act of love.

Eleonora's father, a wealthy farmer and landowner, brought his family to summer in their seaside villa at Partanna Mondello. He liked to cook fish and taught his daughter how to fry when she was very young. But one evening he lost everything in a card game, and later he died in a car crash, leaving large debts. "I loved him so much," she said. Her father's brother raised Eleonora and her three sisters, saw them married, and saved for them a little land near Valguarnera, southwest of Enna, in Caltanisetta province.

In June they played in the middle of wheatfields. "I remember the clang of sheep bells at dusk, the scream of lambs being slaughtered." The sun dried the tomato paste smeared on screens in the piazza and warmed the scent of the basil in pots on the balcony. "These odors have entered our blood." She meant the blood of Sicilians.

Then came the cooling night and the jasmine-scented breeze, "the drunken perfumes." When she and her sisters reached a certain age, around midnight they'd hear a horse's hooves clopping on the cobblestones, then a mandolin playing. Their mother would call up the stairs, "Close all the shutters!" but the girls would pretend to be asleep, and creep to the balcony on their bellies. "We couldn't see who was serenading us, but maybe it's better that way. You can fantasize." Eleonora compiled a book of Sicilian *serenate*, with the music and lyrics illustrated in watercolors.

She started to cook seriously in middle age, after a pioneering career as a woman journalist in print, radio, and television. *La Cucina del Sole* was not the first back-to-the-land Sicilian cookbook, but Eleonora did host the first television show to focus on rustic dishes. The Lions and Rotary clubs all over eastern Sicily asked her to speak at their meetings. Little by little, the love of the traditional Sicilian food spread.

She spent eleven years seeking the "pearls of Sicily"—*Le Perle della Sicilia* was the name of her show—in the island's most overlooked spots. She found a rare woman shepherd who would wake at dawn with a shepherd's crook in her hand, take her sheep to the mountains, milk them, and make cheese. A farmer once taught Eleonora to cook vegetables *in cartuccio,* "in paper." She learned that Sicilians keep pumpkins on their roofs for luck and to hold their roof tiles down when the sirocco blows. Most of the interviews turned into love-fests between the peasants who shared their recipes and Eleonora who valued their stories.

Once Eleonora had to get an archbishop's permission to visit the cloistered Sisters of the Holy Spirit in their convent in Licati (this is the same order that figured in the famous scene in *The Leopard,* in which Don Fabrizio, the prince, pays a visit to the convent). Only four nuns were left in the convent when Eleonora arrived in the nineteen-eighties, and they would not allow her into their kitchen. From her side of the grate Eleonora tried to pry from them the ancient recipe for their prized almond cake, and another one, for a dessert couscous made with candied fruit. The nuns were polite but firm: no recipes.

Eleonora left empty-handed, but she later met a chef who had apprenticed at the convent, where he had learned to make their dessert couscous. He shared the secret with Eleonora, but she never published the recipe, out of respect for the nuns' jealous love.

26

LOVE ON A PLATE

༄

When I'm on the road in Sicily I eat street food. It's cheap, it's good, and it's a way to watch Sicilians. Street food feeds a need in them much deeper than hunger—their need to be close. Sicilians telephone each other from the back of the bus to the front, and seek out the crowded beaches, the piazzas packed with people, and markets where they're likely to get mauled. They must have company, or at least an audience, for whatever they do. In Sicily, where food is love and the street is a stage, street food is more than a cheap meal, it's Communion.

Some of my fondest memories revolve around it. When I lived with Piero in Mondello our piazza had a fountain with a bare-breasted mermaid facing the sea, her arms raised to the sky with a fish in one hand and a seashell in the other. Between her and the turquoise bay there used to be a row of shacks selling *frutti di mare*: octopuses in tanks, pyramids of spiny *ricci*, sea urchins that look like horse chestnuts, raw oysters, steamed clams and purple-blue mussels, all served on hand-painted ceramic platters. At night in the huts on the water's edge, bare light bulbs hung low over steaming pots behind the cooks in their smeared white aprons. At their backs the black cliffs of Capo Gallo and Monte Pelligrino cuddled the moon when it rose shrimp-colored over the sea.

In the evenings Piero and I used to sit outside the Renato Bar beside the mermaid to watch the *palermitani* come out from the city by the hundreds to graze at the seafood shacks. Men and women weighed down with gold and wearing their best shoes dragged their whiny kids by the hand that wasn't holding an ice cream cone. They'd stroll and stop to belly up to a counter and order a plate of *ricci*, seven of them for about five dollars. Leone, who dived for the *ricci* by day, cracked them open at night with a long, sharp knife. It was like cracking geodes—inside the brown shells were the orange star-shaped gonads of the urchin, shiny and wet, which his customers scooped out with a crust of bread.

I didn't eat seafood then, so Piero would walk over to the outdoor *friggeria*, "the fry shop" (it's still there, behind the mermaid), to buy me an *arancino*, a fried rice ball. Or sometimes he brought back a white paper sack of *panelle*, crisp little squares of deep-fried dough made from chickpea flour, to go with my glass of beer.

In the summer Piero was the lifeguard at Mondello Beach. All July and August I sat in his umbrella chair. We didn't have to leave the beach to eat. Every day a tanned, tow-headed boy from the city picked his way through the beach blankets with a cut-glass bowl full of iced coconut slices held at shoulder level, balanced on his upturned palm.

"*Cocco bello!*" he sang out. Piero would wave him down and choose two meaty white chunks, which the boy handed over with pincers. Piero always overpaid him and told him to keep the change. The boy was one of five brothers from a poor family in Palermo, Piero said, and their father was in jail but got released on weekends to work the beach with his family. An older brother sold hot corn on the cob, which Sicilians devoured without butter or salt and which tasted like over-cooked cow corn to me. Another brother trudged the sand with a cooler of iced drinks. The strap dug deep into his bare shoulder and he sang, "*Acqua, aranciata, birra, Coca-Cola, Sp-r-r-r-ite!*"

In the winter I'd take the bus into Palermo to walk through the Vucciria, the old market off the Piazza San Domenico in Via Roma where the specialty is fresh fish but you can buy almost anything edible. Its main street is a narrow, down-sloping canyon bordered by four-story tenements. In late morning, spears of sunlight strike the cherry-red tarps stretched taut above the vendors' stalls. Glossy black slabs of stone shine under their feet, forever wet with melting fish ice. (A Sicilian who says he'll pay you when the Vucciria dries up means when hell freezes over.)

Shoppers shoulder through the fray past mounds of black olives the size of quail eggs and cooked baby artichokes bobbing in cauldrons. Down at the base of the street, I once watched a man in a suit coat and fedora choose a small octopus from a tank, have it boiled, squeeze a lemon over it and eat it for breakfast. In a corner of the cramped piazza two men stood behind a belly-high barrel eating *milza* and washing it down with tumblers of white wine. *Milza* is thinly sliced calf spleen, deep-fried, then drizzled with lard and cheese and served on a bun. They wiped their greasy chins on their shirt-sleeves, laughing and joking in the warm winter sunshine.

There were bushel baskets overflowing with *babbaluci*, tiny white snails that climb over each other trying vainly to escape. In July, during the five-day feast of Santa Rosalia, men deep-fry them with garlic in vats of olive oil on street corners. Revelers suck them out of their shells and chase the tidbits with a bottle of beer.

In the market I watched one man stop at what looked like a plate of glass splinters. He grabbed a fistful, threw his head back and swallowed them. They were *neonati*, transparent newborn fish that Sicilian women steam and sprinkle on pasta but men just eat raw—for virility, the man told me. A fisherman, he liked to scoop *neonati* live from his net, salted by the sea, "and feel them wriggle down my throat."

I preferred *pizzette,* palm-sized pizzas I bought for a dollar in bars or bakeries. They have kept me alive on the road; if I eat one for brunch I'm good until evening.

In Mondello we lived fifty feet from the piazza in a street just one block long. Summer nights, when it was time to eat supper but too hot to cook, Piero would stop at the foot of Via Terza Compagnia to buy boiled potatoes and green beans that Filippo, the greengrocer, had cooked over a gas burner on the

27

THE FEAST OF SAINT AGATHA

ॐ

Mount Etna is awesome and dangerous. The volcano expands and contracts a few inches daily, belching thousands of tons of sulfur dioxide and steam in a streaming white vapor pennant. She spits rocks; one broke the windshield of a passenger jet. The Catania airport closes down when she's active. One sunny day in the city my friend Palmina brought an umbrella to a funeral "because it was raining stones." A 1699 earthquake sent the city's Amenano River underground. It now surfaces briefly at a fountain at the Catania fish market, passes through two conch shells held aloft by life-sized stone mermen, then disappears again under the city, a constant reminder that Etna can change one's destiny in an instant.

Until 1699 the city of Catania was on flat terrain and its river flowed above ground. Then the earth split open and Etna vomited so much lava that it flowed through the city streets thirty miles from the crater. Monte Sangiuliano, the aborted start of a new volcano that never broke the surface to spew molten lava, rose abruptly, creating a steep hill in the city center. During the earthquake the ground swallowed people and houses. The tidal wave that followed inundated a dozen coastal villages. Meanwhile the lava was coating miles of fields, pastures, orchards, and vines. Molten rock filled the moats of Castello Ursino, Catania's eleventh-century fortress, then oozed into the sea. Locals say their coastal fish taste exceptional because they feed on plants that grow only on submerged lava.

In the 1700's, Giuseppe Lanza, the duke of Camastra, rebuilt the city in black-and-white Baroque, creating stately mansions with horseshoe arches made of lava blocks limned with white limestone that lead to leafy interior courtyards. Some façades are stuccoed in tan, burnt pink, and smoked pastel blue. The duke designed a broad boulevard, the Via Etnea, to run in a long straight line from Catania's Piazza Duomo, a stone's throw from the sea, up to Etna's lowest slopes. The boulevard ends with a dramatic view of the volcano, the city's destroyer and creator. In front of the cathedral, the Duomo, stands a fountain with a statue of an ancient black-lava elephant with white limestone tusks, the symbol of the city's longevity, bearing an Egyptian obelisk. The elephant is known as Liotru and his saddle is carved with arcane glyphs. A ring of water jets spray Liotru day and night.

࿔ ࿔ ࿔

No human endeavor can stop a volcano, so Catanians turn for assistance to Sant'Agata (Saint Agatha), a native daughter and virgin Christian martyr who died in 252 at the age of fifteen—mutilated, lacerated, and burned—because she would not marry the pagan proconsul, Quintian, who ruled the then Roman colony. Born, tradition says, to Apolla and Rao on September 8, 235, she grew up Christian in a patrician villa in Via Biscari, a pretty girl of good family. In those days, a girl who consecrated herself to the Christian God took a solemn vow of chastity before her bishop, who gave her a ring, a crown of flowers, and a veil to be placed on her grave when she died. Quintian tortured Christians, but he was supposedly in love with Agatha. First he tried to seduce her with money and luxury, but she refused his advances because she was pledged as a bride of Christ. She wouldn't budge; she too had lived under the volcano.

Her refusal was a personal insult to the consul and an affront to the Roman Empire. Quintian had her arrested in an olive grove and taken to the prison that still extends around Piazza Stesicoro. During her trial she was kept in a cell in the present Sant'Agata al Carcere ("Saint Agatha in prison"). This is where the torture began. They pulled off her breasts with pincers. They poked holes in her sides with hot irons. Still she resisted. On February 3 they enclosed her in a limestone kiln, where she roasted on hot coals. She lived but her body became a bleeding sore. The strong-willed teenager suffered for almost two days before dying on February 5. Her relics are kept in

Catania's cathedral: one of her breasts, parts of her arms, a foot, and her veil. A year to the day after her death, they say, Agatha in heaven saved her native city from a lava flow, the first of many civic-minded miracles. And her silk veil could also work miracles; at least a dozen times, when held up before the lava, it stopped the murderous flow. During the 1699 eruption, they say, a river of lava ripped a wooden icon of Agatha off the city wall and carried it unharmed a hundred yards down Via Cappuccini to rest, intact, in what is now Via Etnea.

Every year on February 4 and 5, the men of Catania pull her relics, housed in bejeweled life-sized effigy, through the streets of Catania for two days and two nights, the duration of her martyrdom. It is said to be the second largest religious procession in the world, after the Corpus Domini procession in Cuzco, Peru, and rivals Holy Week in Seville, Spain. Catanians love Agatha like a sister, like a mother, like a girlfriend. Half the women here are named after her, but it is really a feast for the men, who have claimed the girl saint for their own. The citywide rite unfolds like a collective dream.

By the first of February the colored lights arch over Via Etnea spelling out "*Viva Sant'Agata.*" Nut sellers and nougat makers do a brisk business from their pushcarts near Villa Bellini, the city's elegant park, where a gardener forms the date in flowers. The sweet smoke of caramelized sugar clouds the night air. A public fervor takes over the city. "For a week, everybody is good," said my friend Valentina Bua, who loves living in Catania's historic center.

In the days before the procession, nineteen *candelore*, fifteen-foot-tall wooden towers, are carried out of the churches where they are stored by teams made up of members of the city's guilds. In the procession they will precede the carriage carrying Saint Agatha and her relics. At one time the *candelore* may have been simple lanterns, but for the past few hundred years at least they have been multitiered Baroque towers of carved and gilded wood. Sculpted wood shadowbox figures on each tier tell the tale of Agatha's martyrdom. At the base of each tower are gilded swans, busty seraphim, or the pudgy supporting arms of putti. The *candelore* are fitted with small battery-powered crystal chandeliers. The city's butchers, bakers, carpenters, stonemasons, fishermen, florists, funeral directors, wine merchants, and grocers carry these beautiful burdens on shoulder poles through their own neighborhoods. I saw a motley band of skinny men with gelled hair dressed in black jeans and leather jackets play the trumpet and snare drum before their own *candelora*. Perhaps because the feast comes on the heels of the pagan *Carnevale*, the roving guild bands play anything, from Sicilian folk songs to "When the Saints Go Marching In" to one about a guy and his prostitute girlfriend. Valentina told me the words to its chorus: "She doesn't have sex at night, but all day, all day, all day."

The official two-day procession, unaccompanied by music, begins on February 4 after the dawn Mass in the cathedral. The statue of Saint Agatha that houses her relics is placed on a *fercolo*, a 40,000-pound silver carriage pulled by five thousand men, each of whom wears a white tunic, white gloves, and a black velvet Renaissance hat, the *scuzetta*. The white tunic, the *saio*, has its origins in the rough burlap sacks Byzantine Orthodox Greeks once donned for mourning or doing penitence. The men grasp two long, thick ropes and pull Saint Agatha through the outer and then the inner neighborhoods of Catania, passing the stations of her martyrdom. Melted wax from oversized votive candles coats the streets. Valentina told me, "Five thousand people pull the *fercolo* up Monte Sangiuliano," the would-be volcano in the city center. "Do you know how many people slip and die? They get trampled if they fall. They run up the hill, ambulances at every corner."

One year I came down from Mount Etna to watch the procession. It was raining buckets when I woke at 4:30 A.M. to attend the special dawn Mass, *la Messa dell'Aurora*. With a borrowed umbrella I walked for fifteen minutes in the pitch dark to the Duomo. Via Etnea was a river and all the minor streets tributaries, and all the water was flowing to the cathedral. At each curb it rose over the tops of my boots and soaked my socks. I was still half asleep when I saw a man in a butcher's smock, then another, and another, all heading my way. *Why are all the butchers out walking at this hour?* I wondered. When my mind cleared I realized they were devotees dressed in the *saio*. We all flowed downhill in the dark.

The people and the water pooled up in the Piazza Duomo under Liotru. The devotees stood umbrella to umbrella before the eleventh-century cathedral. It was still dark but hinting at day when the cathedral lit up dusky blue, and majestic organ music swelled from the interior. I stepped inside. The golden *candelore* lined the side aisles of the Duomo. A dozen priests in jewel-colored chasubles celebrated *la Messa dell'Aurora* together. One conducted the singing with his hands, shouting the words before each line. I saw one girl wearing a green tunic and asked her why.

"For the longest time, women couldn't wear any tunic" for the feast of Saint Agatha, she said. But the women had demanded a place in the procession. "The bishop relented and said pious women could participate in the cortege and could wear tunics, but green, not white like the men."

The crowd was so thick I couldn't see above the heads, but a man gave me his place on the side altar steps. "She's just come out now," he said. Suddenly, the women shouted, "Look! Look! How beautiful she is." They pressed their hankies to their cheeks and cried while the men sang and waved their own accordion-pleated hankies.

Agatha rose slowly and glittering from her subterranean vault. First her crown, then her smiling face, then her shoulders and the silver-winged angels at her elbows. She was fair-skinned and blonde. The life-sized effigy was of Saint Agatha down to her hips. Her head appeared to be of carved and painted wood. Her hair fell loose to her shoulders. Her cheeks were pink and plump with girlish fat, but she smiled like a woman who'd walked through fire.

Her jewel-encrusted gold crown, which weighs more than two pounds, was given to her by Richard the

Lionhearted of England in 1190. It is set with diamonds and rubies the size of small eggs. Her robe is covered with gold filigree, brooches, and 250 large precious stones, including ten large emeralds. She wears rings on every finger, including one with nineteen diamonds. In the fifteenth century the Spanish viceroy Ferdinando Acugna draped a massive gold necklace around her neck. In 1881 Queen Margherita of Savoy presented her a ring. Vincenzo Bellini, the opera composer and a native son of Catania, gave her his Cross of the Knights of the Legion of Honor. Agatha still wears most of these, but many of the pounds of gold on her have been the gifts of people like those in the cathedral that day. The women cried into their hankies; the men shouted, *"Viva Sant'Agata! O! Sant'Agata, la gloria!"* She was in this room with them.

Waves of applause rippled through the church as men carried her to the altar. The cathedral was thronged; I could hardly breathe. I broke into an acrid sweat. "Patroness and protectress of our city, pray for us," the priest intoned. When Mass was over, men hoisted her onto their shoulders and walked slowly down the main aisle. The crowd rushed to beat her into the piazza. The press through the door was frightening. I was lifted off my feet. My umbrella snagged on someone or something and got trampled by the crowd. Outside I found a spot out of the rain under the eaves of a bank and waited for whatever would come next. The elephant fountain gushed in my ears. The *fercolo* was parked at the cathedral's front door, decked high and low with pink flowers that symbolized a martyr's blood, ready to take Agatha on her annual ride through the city.

A three-wheeled maintenance truck parked in front of me, blocking my view. People were climbing up into its cargo bed to get a better look and keep their feet dry. Saro Iugulano, fifty-six, who wore the uniform of a city maintenance man, gave me a hand up and found me a spot under someone's umbrella. "When I was young I brought my six-month-old son to see the *festa*," he said. "Oh, the press of the crowd in Via Etnea!" His son went home with no hat, no shoes, and one ripped sleeve. He promised him he'd see the *festa* again when he could walk on his own and protect himself. "You are lucky it's raining. If it were not for the bad weather, this piazza would be a carpet of people."

At 7 A.M. a bell tolled twice. "This is the time when the saint usually comes out," Saro said. He had to get to work moving barriers around. I went back to my spot under the eaves and stood next to a tall young man with shoulder-length black hair dressed in the *saio* and *scuzetta*. His name was Giuseppe Riscica, and he came from a small town on the outskirts of Catania.

Besides protection from Etna, Agatha grants personal favors. When prayers are answered, the halt find spouses, the barren give birth, tumors shrink, the grandson beats his heroin habit, you dream the winning numbers. I asked Giuseppe why he wore the *saio*.

"When I was sixteen, I had a problem, and I resolved it successfully." (It is bad luck to say what you prayed for.) "I decided to wear the *saio* every year for the rest of my life, and I named my son Agatino," he said.

At 7:25, the bells tolled and fireworks boomed in solemn rhythms. Saint Agatha was borne into the piazza. Giuseppe let fall tidbits of lore about the saint. "She is kept locked in a great room ten meters below ground, with alarms. Only the archbishop and the prefect have the keys, and both must be used at the same time.

"Ninety percent of the time it rains for the *festa*," he said. "She is angry because of the goddess."

"What goddess?" I asked.

The goddess was Isis, the city's last fertility deity, whose image once stood in a neighborhood called the Borgo. During the desperate years of a drought in a bygone century, Christians had prayed to this Isis for rain, making Agatha so jealous that since then she has made it rain every year for the Dawn Mass.

The men shouldering the *candelore* used to bet on who could make it to the top of Monte Sangiuliano all in one run. The men pulling the saint in her *fercolo* up this steep route make sure they are positioned near dear friends, because devotees tearing up the hill will trample anyone who has slipped on the spilled candle wax and fallen. "You must be with people who will drag you along with the ropes," Giuseppe said.

At 8 A.M. the cathedral bells pealed wildly. I heard singing. It rained harder. Men in the crowd were yelling, calling out for prayers: "*Cittadini! Cittadini!* For Saint Agatha, lovely and miraculous, are we all devoted, all of us? *Siamo tutti devoti tutti?*"

"*Certo! Certo! Viva Sant'Agata! Viva Sant'Agata!*"

It was a refrain I would hear repeated for the next forty-eight hours. Six men in smocks lifted the saint into her carriage and climbed on to ride shotgun with two priests. Everywhere men with pushcarts sold five-foot yellow candles that people bought and passed up to the men on the wagon who lit them with another candle. The carriage was ablaze. Thousands of men took up positions on the long cords, and the *fercolo* made a turn of the piazza, then headed toward the sea under the arch of the Porta Uzeda. Giuseppe and I fell in. He grabbed on to a rope and I walked in front of him and behind his buddy, Giacomo. They didn't seem to mind the rain. Giacomo told me, "The left rope is one hundred thirteen meters long, the right rope one hundred five." This is because of the left turn they have to make after they run up Monte Sangiuliano. Just then someone yelled *"Cittadini!"*— "Citizens!"—and the men murmured, *"Viva Sant'Agata!"* and beat their shoulders with their gloves like a scourge.

"*Cittadini!*" he screamed again.

"*Viva Sant'Agata.*"

"Let us call to her with grace and heart. *Siamo tutti devoti tutti?*"

"*Certo! Certo!*" the chorus shouted.

The men who called out for the prayers did so randomly and spontaneously. Whenever one would yell he tried to be the loudest. His friends would brace their arms against the small of his back so he could arch backward and shout from his diaphragm.

The procession would move along for a few yards, then stop. The pace was glacial. "How do you know when to stop pulling?" I asked Giuseppe.

"The *fercolo* has brakes."

A city tow truck led the procession, ready to remove obstacles, then came police cars, a ladder truck to lift low-hanging wires, and candle sellers pushing wheeled racks of swinging yellow tapers. Behind them, nineteen teams of mostly potbellied men with cowls on their heads carried their *candelore* on shoulder poles, crouching under the weight, waddling forward from their hips, tiny crystal chandeliers tinkling. The rain tapered off and the gold towers shone dully under the gray sky. The signal to stop the tower bearers for a rest is two knocks on the wooden shaft from the *candelora*'s team captain. The men would set the load down in synchrony, then squat on their heels to stretch their backs.

The saint, carrying a gold scepter topped by an emerald-studded cross, followed the line of *candelore* at a languid, Sicilian cadence, resting often. Behind her trailed more candle sellers, the ambulance, balloons, nut vendors, and a growing crowd of the faithful out for a walk with their best girl, Agatha. We had stopped partly because the *candelore* preceding the carriage had stopped, partly because the men on the *fercolo* were collecting candles and money from the public. Men and women along the route darted in to touch the two three-inch-diameter ropes. Small boys were allowed to grasp the loop handles at the ends of the ropes. "Their fathers want to give them a sense of what it is like, to make them feel grown up," Giuseppe said. We passed first through the Civitá, where Agatha grew up, now a poor fishermen's quarter. A chorus of girls sang to Agatha on a street corner. People handed their babies up to have them touch the saint.

As we passed under an arch, printed paper strips fluttered down. I opened my hand and one fluttered into it. "WW Sant'Agata" was written on it. "*Viva.*" When it was time to pull again, the man in charge of the *fercolo* rang a set of silver altar bells. A strange quiet reigned except for the irregular and often distant shouting of the men to their saint. I walked in silence, Giuseppe behind me and Giacomo ahead. "She is protected," he said to his friend, and that is how I felt. After a few hours they left to pick up Giuseppe's son. He gave me his cell phone number and a way to find him later in this sea of white smocks: "Just remember, I'll always be on the left rope."

At noon there was a long stop. I bought a sandwich and beer in a deli and sat on its stoop to eat it. A man sat down next to me. Each section of the procession route is dear to someone. "The most beautiful thing is the ascent at the Carmelite convent," he said. I went back to my friend Palmina's to sleep a few hours so I could stay awake that night.

At night the *fercolo* looked like a fiery ghost wagon, with hundreds of candles that flickered and flared in the faces of the six men manning it: two to tend candles, two to take flowers, two to collect money. They took turns touching babies to Agatha. People passed bills up to the handsome young priest in his pink stole and white alb. He stuffed the money into one of four gray flannel-covered boxes at the rear of the carriage.

Alfio Rao, forty-five, captained the *fercolo*. "You need a lot of guts," he told a reporter for *La Sicilia*. For two days he commands five thousand men who have never trained together, and takes responsibility for the lives of spectators who line the streets and for the city's sweetheart, Saint Agatha. He stands without reins, like the warrior on the tarot deck's Chariot card driving his pair of sphinxes outside the city gate. He dons the *saio* because twice he survived burnings, once when he was two and a pot of hot water spilled on him, and again at age five when he caught fire. The *fercolo*'s two brakemen ride unseen and unseeing below his feet. Rao signals them electronically and by jingling the bells, once for "go," twice for "slow," and continuous ringing for "stop." The *fercolo*'s wheels can turn forty-five degrees; for sharper turns four men hidden in the chassis hoist it on a turn screw and revolve it. The wait at some corners seemed endless.

About six-thirty that evening they arrived at the hill of the Carmelite convent, near the site of Agatha's jail cell and Quintian's private quarters. The men pulling on the ropes rested and waited for the order to pull the carriage—and all the men on it; the blazing candles; the pink flowers; the silver, gold, and jewels; the saint's flesh; and the money—up the steep rise and round a bend. Children hung like monkeys on the monastery fence. A crowd clogged the narrow street. Palmina brought her son and daughter to watch.

On a signal, thousands of men charged up the hill like wild horses. Alfio Rao wrapped one arm around a column and hung out from the *fercolo* whipping his gloves at the men on the ropes and yelling madly, "Go! GO!" Agatha whisked by like a teenager on a joyride. The scene was short but worth the wait. The ascent of Monte Sangiuliano would be five times longer and twice as steep.

The next stop was Sant'Agata al Carcere. I stood at the base of the church's sloping black wall behind the smoke of roasting chestnuts. A dark haggard Gypsy woman with thinning black hair pulled tight into a bun suckled a boy on the bottom step. With her right hand she held out an empty plastic tray to passersby.

I waited outside with Agatha when we came to Sant'Agata al Vetere, which was the city's cathedral before the Duomo was built. Her remains were first kept there. The church had thrown open its three front doors and song and light from the chandeliers spilled out into the night. The *fercolo* blazed with candles that lit up the lava walls and basalt paving stones. When it moved again the procession slipped smoothly through the streets like an arm through a black satin sleeve.

The streets were alive and the cafés were full of the faithful. The horse butchers set up grills outside their shops and the smoke of roasted meat rose up to those who leaned on their balcony rails and looked down on the lights, the sea of white robes, the men looking very Botticelli in their black velvet hats. Along the procession path street vendors sold pistachios, walnuts, peanuts, hazelnuts, and chickpeas roasted over coals. Bands of roaming teenage girls in tight flared pants, white jackets, white scarves, and painted-on black eyeliner were summarily ignored by boys in white smocks whose thoughts were only of Agatha.

Groups of friends pulled the *fercolo* through the streets all night. I took out my tape recorder and asked a group of twenty-somethings if I could record them. Luca, Salvo, Gianluca, Giuseppe, Sebastiano, Davide, and Dario took turns screaming to Sant'Agata, one outdoing the next in volume. Gianluca's face turned red and his neck muscles bulged when he leaned back into the arms of comrades and screamed to the sky, "Saint Agatha, beautiful and miraculous! Are we all devotees all of us? *Siamo tutti devoti tutti?*"

"*Certo, certo,*" murmured the rest, whipping themselves with their handkerchiefs. Again, in a hoarse squeak, exhausted, in some kind of frenzy, he piped, "Louder still! *Cittadini! Cittadini! Siamo tutti devoti tutti?*"

Sometimes ten or more of them would go down on their knees in an impromptu prayer circle inside the two ropes, vying to shout the loudest. They seemed possessed. Catania is not a town noted for its feminism. Do they do this because Agatha defended her virginity to the death? Because she refused every bribe? Because she was strong and proud like a real man?

The procession carried on all night, but I fell into bed at two in the morning and woke to bombs at a quarter to six.

Agatha had arrived at Porta Uzeda. I dressed in a flash and ran down into Via Etnea in the dark. A policeman assured me, "The saint has not yet arrived home." When she did, she'd spend the day, a night, and the following day in the cathedral, then go out again just after dusk the next night. Police were clearing the street because she would arrive running.

After the grueling trek the devotees ran through the city gate in a mad dash to park the *fercolo* in front of the cathedral while red and green fireworks burst in the predawn dark. The men had no voice, spoke in squeaks and with sign language. The money bags were the first thing off the *fercolo*. The cathedral bells were pealing.

The largest bell is called Agatha; as it rang I could see its clapper, which alone weighs three hundred pounds. Legend says that during one of the bell's recastings the faithful tossed in their gold and silver and their sacrifices account for the bell's sweet C note. At nearly nine tons it is the fifth largest bell in Italy, the tenth largest in the world. Once an earthquake sent it flying to the seashore, but it didn't crack. It was last redesigned and recast in 1614 and decorated with a frieze depicting the history of Catania. Inscribed on it in Latin are the words:

I cast out demons.
I calm the storms.
I call to the living.
I cry for the dead.

Now the bells rang for joy. A man passed his silver Saint Agatha Society medallion up to a priest in a magenta robe, who blessed it. The men on the *fercolo* passed pink flowers down to people in the crowd. Tomorrow the flowers would be white, symbolizing Agatha's apotheosis. One man climbed onto the carriage, pointed at Agatha, and called to the crowd, "Isn't she beautiful? Are we all devotees?"

"*Certo! Certo!*" Their voices had been reduced to hisses. Other church bells rang in the distance. Men shouted hoarsely and applauded as Agatha was lifted off the *fercolo*, sparkling in the blue dawn light. An old man took off his gloves and gazed at her, drinking her in. He made the sign of the cross and kissed his fingertips.

"*Siamo tutti devoti tutti?*" The last shout.

"*Cittadini! Cittadini!*"

Then silence. Men who pulled her all night touched their hankies to the saint. I stared at her back as she floated above our heads down the cathedral's nave, slowly, like a Norman queen under the pointed Arab arches. Spanking applause echoed off the church walls. When she reached the altar she turned around and faced the congregation as a fleshy girl, smiling and full of health. She stood under a crucifix lit by twelve long white tapers. People grouped around her and stared as I did. When I moved my head from side to side sparkling dewdrops of violet and green danced on her jewels. A blinding white diamond light shone at her shoulder. On her breast she wore a two-inch-wide poppy-red coral cabochon. The topaz stone in her crown above her third eye sent out a yellow beam. She was glorious. An amazing silence fell in the half-full church.

When Mass was over the captain of the *fercolo* appeared in civvies and shook the hand of the priest in the purple stole. Outside, the Piazza Duomo had already emptied, the barriers were stowed, and I blinked at Etna, blinding white in a veil of new snow.

⁂ ⁂ ⁂

It was already dark when I arrived in the Piazza Duomo at about 5:30 P.M. the next afternoon, for the start of the second part of the procession. It was already dark. Sawdust filled the cracks between the cobblestones so people could get some purchase on the wax-speckled street. Flanking my path for blocks before the cathedral, men stood next to enormous seven-wick candles. The largest candle weighed 220 pounds and stood as tall as the man who carried it. Some devotees pledge to shoulder these all night, and some just for a stretch of the Via Etnea. They gathered in groups, trimming their wicks, dumping the excess wax in the street. Once when Palmina was pregnant she slipped on the wax. "Now they scrape the streets with snow shovels after the procession," she said. Still, some two thousand traffic accidents occur in Catania the day after the feast. No one would dare to make a law eliminating the giant candles.

The seven-wick torches were made at two Catania waxworks by fusing seven smaller candles together; they gave off heat, and people lit their cigarettes at the flames and warmed their palms, their faces lit up orange. The giant candles lined both sides of Via Etnea, each as bright as a campfire. Shadows jumped and shrank impetuously on the city's Baroque walls. The ropes were stretched out before the *fercolo*, now once again parked in front of the cathedral. The flowers were white now because Agatha had died and gone to heaven. This was her triumph. The bells pealed solemnly; I was nearly crushed by the crowd in Piazza Duomo. At five-forty the bells rang wildly. Boys in white robes shouted, "*Siamo tutti devoti tutti?*" and pink and white fireworks lit the ultramarine sky over the cathedral. When the sky turned blue velvet the *fercolo* moved off slowly with a hundred ten-pound candles blazing, as Agatha was hauled up the boulevard toward Etna.

The mountain was a geyser of fire but Agatha smiled at it. We couldn't hear the explosions that showered sparks on the summit but we saw the silent fountain spouting magma that dribbled in orange rivulets down the mountain's flanks. The bearers of giant candles did a slalom through the crowd. Along the way, little boys sold slices of citron with a pinch of salt to slake thirst.

The procession would pass under Valentina's second-story balcony, so she threw an open-house party and I went. Her apartment was a few yards from Piazza Borgo, where the Isis statue had last been worshiped. The procession traditionally makes a long stop there and men set up a tremendous display of fireworks sometime in the middle of the night. Now I was the one leaning safely on a balcony rail. The street filled with the smell of fat dripping on hot coals and melted yellow wax. The crowd below was a carpet of heads. We saw the two parallel lines of pullers pass below us, the only discernible current. We stood on the balcony with paper cups of wine and watched Agatha loom into sight a hundred yards down the wide avenue, wobbling behind all nineteen *candelore* and the sluggish river of flames. She had made her way up the boulevard from the cathedral, past the sunken Roman amphitheater, the swans at Bellini Park, and the designer stores in Via Etnea; now she came into the Borgo, where she would rest awhile.

At almost every intersection now, the *fercolo* was met by a dump truck parked in a side street. Valentina and I watched for forty minutes while the men took the candles from the crowd, passed them behind the saint, then threw them into the dump truck on the other side. The Church sold the used candles back to the waxworks, I was told, which made and sold new ones as fast as they could. The saint had stopped directly under our balcony, so we could see that the *fercolo's* roof was covered with tiny chased silver skulls. Valentina ran down to offer two candles of her own; her mother had discovered a lump in her breast. When she came back one of the crowd below us fainted and someone shouted for sugar, which Valentina threw down in a bag. Another person fainted and in three minutes the first-aid crew had found her. The *fercolo* hadn't moved for more than an hour.

"They don't want to put Agatha away," Valentina explained. "The night is clear and tomorrow is Sunday. People can sleep all day when it's over. Last year she came home at ten on a Monday morning, then the people went to work."

Valentina conferred with two friends and me. We had to decide whether to see the dangerous ascent of Monte Sangiuliano or hear the song of the cloistered Franciscan nuns, the Poor Clares, when they sang a cappella to the saint. Because of the crowd, it is nearly impossible to see both. We decided on the song because I didn't want to see anybody get killed. We napped for two hours and then at 3 A.M. we ate Pocket Coffees, chocolates filled with coffee syrup, and followed our friend Luisa up side-street staircases to Via Crociferi, site of most of Catania's monasteries and convents. The *fercolo* was not expected for hours, but people clogged this narrow lane three deep on either side. One man climbed over a fence into the courtyard of the Benedictine convent, whose Mother Superior came out and shooed him away. People clung to cornices and ledges. Devotee bouncers made a gangway for the *fercolo*. My back was pressed against a railing around an abandoned archaeological dig where researchers had uncovered the walls of the Roman city, then had run out of money. I climbed down and stood on a wall of thin red bricks with my arm hooked through the guardrail, looking through the legs of my friends and waiting for the saint.

A covered causeway arched over the street to connect the Poor Clares with the Benedictine convent. Veiled silhouettes shifted behind the passageway's barred windows. "They are the cloistered nuns, looking for the first sign of the *fercolo*," Valentina said. "Once day breaks they will not go to the window."

Saint Agatha arrived just as the first pink rays of dawn hit the Benedictine convent. The mother superior presented flowers to the archbishop of Catania, who placed them on Agatha's catafalque. Then came the part that Alfio Rao liked the best: "Thirty thousand people in absolute silence listening to hymns. What shivers!" The Poor Clares sang in Latin from behind their bars, then silently tossed flower petals onto the saint.

As the *fercolo* passed, a man on it handed my friend Adriana a handful of holy cards that had been touched to the saint's effigy. She gave me one, which I later taped into my address book, which was the only item in my knapsack with my name and phone number in it. Days later, I left the bag in a taxi I took out of Newark airport. Before I realized it was missing, the cabbie had turned it in with my camera, tape recorder, wallet, film, notes, credit cards, and cash intact. He never responded to my offer of a reward.

Via Crociferi was just a few blocks from the Duomo, which was the end of the road for Agatha, but we knew she'd take hours to get there. We women decided to get breakfast, then wait for Agatha at the cathedral.

The men brought her home just before noon, but they hated to see her go. White gloved hands reached out to touch her. In a thunder of fireworks and ringing bells they sent her down to her dark vault. Outside, work crews had already taken down the festival lights and devotees were eating brioches stuffed with shaved almond ice. There was sawdust in the street, and the sun was on my back.

28

KEEP IT LIKE THIS

ॐ

RETURNING TO A FAMILIAR PLACE is part of the pleasure of travel for me. In midwinter I checked into the three-room Pensione Itria in the Arab quarter, the oldest part of Polizzi Generosa, my favorite town in the central Madonie Mountains. Signora Albanese gave me a second-floor room. My balcony gave me a view into a kitchen window across the street and down into the life on the bumpy cobblestones below.

"There is another guest," Signora Albanese said. "Marco Galliano. You will meet him." He was twenty-six years old, heir to a baron's palace and to the Galliano palace in Polizzi. As soon as he saw me in the hallway he stuck to me like a wet suit. He was pallid and short with a prominent aristo-cratic nose; I could see blue veins under his cheeks. His hair was sparse, as though he'd suffered from some long illness; he had most of a mustache and was trying to grow a goatee. He spoke in a small voice and muttered to himself. He lived with his parents and sister in Palermo, where he worked for a graphic design firm, he said. The family spent summers in their eighteenth-century palace next to Count Ruggero's cathedral, but when Marco came alone in the winter, his parents wouldn't give him the keys. Like a puppy starved for attention, he dogged me. I wanted some time alone with Polizzi.

"I'm going to unpack and go for a walk."

"I'll come with you," he said.

We walked the western ridge toward La Commenda, the ruins of the most beautiful church in town, which the Knights of Malta built of golden stone in the twelfth century. Marco wore his sunglasses even in late winter. "I have fair skin, and blue blood," he said. "The Gallianos came from Naples, descended from the first Spanish Bourbons. The Book of Gold shows the lineage." The Book of Gold is a catalogue of Italian aristocrats. We stopped at the western edge of town, where we could see the sun going down behind jagged blue peaks across the valley. A grounded cloud crept up the steep greensward toward our feet. The sun's horizontal rays kindled the mist from within, tingling the grass, the rocks, and the air with warm orange light. I stood still to burn the scene into my memory. Marco put one trembling hand on my arm and wiped his nose with his other sleeve.

"It's the first night of *Carnevale*," Signora Albanese had said. "You should go to the town dance at the Cinema Cristallo." Marco and I walked side by side in the dark, wrapped up against the wind. I watched the tapestry scroll under my feet. Pastel confetti stuck to the wet stones. In Polizzi, the Corso Garibaldi was paved with plain basalt, but Via Roma had repeated blocks of patterns inlaid with two smooth strips of red brick where cartwheels once rolled smoothly. These streets had texture, pattern, and color and showed the touch of the human hand. Many had been covered with asphalt, but the town had since passed a law requiring new streets to be made of stone and the old roadbeds to be exposed. A kid in a clown suit squirted an aerosol stream of blue foam on Marco. The child's father egged him on: "Go, GO!" All the rules get broken during *Carnevale*.

At 10 P.M. the crowd at the dance hall was still sparse. We paid for our tickets and went in to one big room with a wood floor, a stage, tiers of folding theater seats, and a projection screen rolled up above the stage. A band was setting up. People in costume wore plastic bags on their feet so their shoes wouldn't give them away. Nana was right: people know you by your shoes.

A masked girl in a pink chiffon dress scuffed around the floor wielding a giant orange bat. Balloons dangled from the ceiling. "They open this place only for parties and holidays," Marco said. "They don't show films here anymore."

The two-man band struck up. Between them they played accordion, sax, clarinet, electric piano, and drum machine. A couple danced the polka, whirling counterclockwise around the room. Two little kids in masks and plastic feet spun with them. They learn how to dance from their parents who danced in their kitchens when they were growing up.

Around midnight people of all ages trickled in—teenagers, kid brothers, fiancés, married couples, babes in arms, grand-parents.

"Do you want to dance?" Marco asked.

"Let's walk up to the Orto dei Cappuccini and come back later."

My friend Giovanna Galiota had taken me to the Capucin Garden restaurant five years before. Its brick-vaulted kitchen was once part of a monastery and the rest was newly built of stone on what was once the friars' kitchen garden. I remembered the wooden door in a high courtyard wall and the fig tree that grew in the stone-paved patio. It was a misty spring night; we had a corner table under an open window. A fire burned in the stone hearth, wooden arches spanned the Gothic ceiling. A thread of fog floated through the window and took the form of a finger pointing to our table.

Five years later I navigated my way back to the restaurant with Marco. A man stood in the walled patio with his hands in his pockets, looking like a spider waiting for flies.

"Are you the owner?" I asked.

"Sì."

"You probably don't remember me, but I'm—"

"You are Theresa Maggio. Come inside."

He led us in. He took me by the elbow into the room to the left and pointed to the table by the window. "You ate with Giovanna and you sat at that table. You had pasta with gor-gonzola sauce. You were wearing pink shoes."

"I don't own any pink shoes."

"They were pink. They looked like house slippers."

Oh, God. The beaded moccasins.

His name was Santo Lipani and he had waited on Giovanna and me but I didn't remember him, just the finger of fog. Now he handed us each a *limoncello* and we all three put our feet up at the fire.

I told Santo how much I liked his town.

"If you've been here so often, why haven't you come to the restaurant?"

"I can't generally afford to eat out. I eat pizzette," I said, and played an invisible violin. He laughed.

When Marco and I decided to walk back to the dance, Santo said, "I'll close the restaurant and come with you."

Now I was beginning to feel like the Pied Piper. At one in the morning the Cinema Cristallo was packed tight and warm with bodies. Couples in costume danced shoulder to shoulder in a slow pinwheel sweep around the room. The ones in the middle just twirled. The kids were as excited as if it were Christmas Eve. I was taking notes. "Come to dinner tomorrow at the restaurant," Santo said.

"Sorry, I can't," I said. "Signora Albanese invited me to her son's birthday dinner tomorrow." Her son, Enzo, would be twenty-two years old.

"We are closed Mondays. Come Tuesday. Come whenever you want."

The next morning was Sunday. When Marco went to Mass I walked to the wide empty piazza at the end of Corso Garibaldi. Everyone else was in church. Polizzi Generosa rides the ridge of a long mountain. From afar it looks like the town is at the helm of a giant ship. I was standing at the prow looking down a thousand feet on green fields dotted with stone farmhouses, diagonal lines of hazelnut trees, twisted black stumps of vines, and scattered almond trees in bloom. New snow had fallen on Monte dei Cervi. On the valley floor an intermittent stream paralleled the Palermo–Catania highway, where the cars were slow-moving colored specks. The first time I saw these mountains, in 1986, I was on my way to Catania in a car that passed right under this peak. I had slouched down in my seat to be able to see up to the top and wondered what life was like up there. I didn't know then that I was looking at Polizzi.

Now I was a speck on the cliff to those below. Mass was over. Behind me toddlers in costume and whiteface paraded around the stone square holding their fathers' hands because their mothers were home making lasagne for dinner. *What peace*, I thought. I heard sheep bleating, the *choof* of a hoe striking earth, and the buzz of a distant chain saw. Boys skateboarded over the piazza stones. Men in caps and capes leaned on their elbows and looked over the stone railing, some at the vista, some at a boys' game of soccer in a playground thirty feet below. I felt the breath of spring. *This town is blessed*, I thought.

ॐ   ॐ   ॐ

At dinner time I walked the scenic route home through Piazza Il Segreto, where two squat palms guard the entrance to the Carpinello Palace. The Roman numerals of a sundial were engraved above the lintel. Men and women bid me *"Buon giorno"* in passing. A canary sang, sparrows twittered, the church bells tolled noon. I stopped in the sequestered courtyard of the Hospital of the Do-Good Brothers in Saint John of God Street—a street all of ten feet long. A priest came out, fed two waiting orange cats, greeted me, and went back inside. I felt perfect happiness.

The birthday dinner at the Pensione Itria was held in a street-level room. Enzo Sauza, Signora Albanese's husband (Sicilian women keep their maiden names in marriage), greeted me at the door and waved his arm at the twenty-six place settings. Three long tables were covered with red and white cloths set under the low vaulted ceiling. I squeezed in among some cousins and aunts. Plump cherubs crawled under the tables and were randomly pulled up onto laps and called "My joy!" They had light, clear complexions and ruddy cheeks. Any one of them could have posed for a Renaissance painting of the Christ child. The white stone room reverberated with the happy family din. I felt caught in a Sicilian Norman Rockwell; it was a scene too good to be true. If there were feuds, those prone to sparring had called a truce for this feast.

Three women in aprons manned the stoves and made the children stay seated when the barrage of abundance began. The first dish was clams in lemon sauce over spaghetti. Then lasagne baked in the brick oven with local ricotta and mushrooms from the surrounding woods. "These are Ferla mushrooms," the woman sitting next to me said. The men at my table named the wild mushrooms they loved to find and eat.

Royal porcino, beech mushrooms, pepper mushrooms, field mushrooms, cabbage mushrooms, citron mushrooms, chestnut mushrooms, pine mushrooms. Every tree gives its different flavor to the fungus. Polizzi's *basilisco* mushrooms are as prized as truffles and grow only at the end of April and into May.

Next came roast pork in cream sauce with carrots, potatoes, onions, and celery served on painted ceramic platters. Then pork ribs in a bowl with potatoes and sweet onions roasted whole and tasting of the coals they were cooked in. Salad was tender lettuce drizzled with vinegar and sprinkled with sea salt. The wine was homemade, golden pink, pungent and warming. My Italian improved right away.

The birthday boy's grandfather said, "The family gets together like this every Sunday." His wife said, "No. Half every week. Every other week, the other half comes. But this is a special occasion." We dug in and there was silence for a few minutes. Signore Sauza said that the *pensione* was a part of Baron Carpinello's house, which I'd passed an eighth of a mile away. "This was the baron's kitchen," he said. "Once it was all one building from here to the baron's residence." The Carpinellos, the Gallianos, the Signorinos, and the Rampollis were four major noble families who kept palaces here in the cool clean air of Polizzi. Now only the Galliano palace is still used by its original owners, for summer vacation. While we spoke, plates of fennel appeared, then platters of fruit arrived soon after: dwarf apples, oranges with the leaves attached, split sun-dried figs. A grandfather made his grandson a sandwich of a roasted hazelnut slipped between two fig halves and handed it to the boy. "Once we used to eat dried figs on bread, like bread and onions, so as not to eat only bread," he said.

"These are things people don't appreciate anymore," Signore Sauza said.

The children were getting restless and couldn't sit still; all their cousins were there to play with. The lights went out and the people parted for the glow of candles on the birthday cake, frosted with whipped cream and decorated with orange slices and coffee beans. Sauza's son blew out twenty-two candles. He'd just finished his military service and now he was home.

"In this cantina room is all that is dear to me," Enzo Sauza said. He crossed his fingers and raised them: "To keep it like this."

29

WATER IN THE STONE

ॐ

In Sperlinga I had spent a night in a sheetrocked cave and sipped coffee in a wood-paneled cavern, but the town's modern troglodytes were still on my mind. How odd to live in a cavity in a monolith, a hobbit hole with a wooden door hung on a rounded opening. What was life there like before wainscoting and TV? How did the people spend their days?

When I called my friend Rita, the Sperlinga tax collector who'd let me sleep in her inherited cave, she told me she'd bought a new cave—one larger and less refined. "You'll like it," she said. So now I was back in the central Nebrodi Mountains in Sicily's northeast, writing by candlelight in a new cave.

The candle was stuck cockeyed in a mayonnaise jar on the floor, dripping wax on the bare stone. The walls were chiseled, rough and black with Bronze Age soot. In the dim light I saw niches chipped into them. It was mid-March in the mountains, but this hole in the cliff was warm. When I undressed I cast a long shadow on the front wall. My shade curved into the ceiling and recoiled over me.

I had arrived in Sperlinga after dark. It was raining and a thick fog had followed my bus from Polizzi Generosa. I met Rita at her apartment in town and ate dinner with her and her children. Her son Fabio, who had grown into a teenager, showed me his ever-growing collection of rocks. He took one clear crystal out of the shoebox, flicked a lighter beneath it, and told me to hush and listen. The crystal crackled then fogged. "There's water trapped in the stone," he said. Heated, it turned to steam and fractured the rock.

His younger sister Nadia, willowy and dark, in her third year of middle school, was a prima ballerina and cross-country champion who planned to study science. Their father, Ahmed, sold fine tablecloths and household linens at the local street markets. It was the Muslim Feast of Abraham, and he and his friends had slaughtered a sheep and were holding a dinner of their own. Ahmed had taught Nadia to count to twenty in Arabic. She made the numbers sound as soothing as a trickling stream.

When it was time for bed Rita gathered a blanket and sheets and drove me to the cliff face. We walked the smooth, narrow serpentine path down staircases that were now mere ripples in the rock. The wind blew the rain sideways. While Rita looked for the key I saw that the lady in the cave next door was up watching television. Her beagle was chained and barking under her wash, which waved limp in the rain.

Inside, the temperature was more comfortable than in my room at the *pensione* in Polizzi. "The rock produces heat," Rita said. I put my hand on the wall and felt warmth. "They had it good," she said, meaning the people who once lived here. "They were warm in the winter and cool in the summer."

Fabio now used this cave as a clubhouse. Rita clicked on a flashlight hung from a bent nail in the rock ceiling. The light swung and shadows leaped on the cavern walls while we put sheets on the clubhouse couch. When Rita left I lit the candle, turned off the flashlight, got into bed, wrote in my journal, blew out the candle, and was alone. I felt like a seed, curled up in a black velvet quiet. I wondered in the dark about the people who were born here, grew up, made love in this spot, worked to eat, and died here. When I awoke, I couldn't remember my dreams.

The morning light entered through a frosted glass door with an iron grating. I sat up and looked around. The room was about seventeen feet wide and was cut twenty-two feet into the mountain, irregularly shaped. The walls were dulled by smoke, but some fresh white-yellow sandstone was exposed where mold had crumbled it into powdery piles. A ball of pooled iron was embedded in the ceiling. For furniture there was a broken stool, a bucket seat from a vehicle, a tube radio, and a wax-splotched picnic table littered with pieces of board games and Sicilian playing cards. On the bumpy wall a white Nike swoosh logo was painted on a field of blue. Plastic dinosaurs were tucked into every niche.

I dressed and headed out; I needed a bathroom and a cappuccino. I walked down the cliff path to the Bar Santa Liberata, named for a protectress of Sperlinga, the only virgin martyr I know of who died crucified. There was a "No Smoking" sign on the wall of the bar, and all the ashtrays were full of butts. The brigadier of the *carabinieri* was reading the pink sports pages and started a yelling match with other customers about the poor management of certain soccer teams. I plugged my ears. The bartender said, "Signorina, don't pay any attention, they're only talking about soccer. They'll calm down after a while."

≈ ≈ ≈

Later that afternoon, Rita introduced me to a man who had grown up in the cave I slept in. Giovanni Mancuso looked to be in his late seventies, and had lived there in the 1920's and '30's. He didn't tell me about how his eyes must have burned in the smoke-filled room, or how crowded it was, with no privacy; he remembered the best of cave life. "Evenings, we danced," he said. "In that little bit of space we danced." Four couples would gather in one cave and dance by candlelight and oil lamps. They couldn't afford musical instruments so they danced to singing and clapping. They played the Jew's harp the whole night. They ate. He gave me his recipe for Sperlinga *sfinge*, a sugar-sprinkled *Carnevale* pastry made from flour, egg, and oil beaten till foamy, then deep-fried until golden. "There was more fun than there is today. Now people sit in front of the television and there is nothing."

When Mancuso was a young man, during *Carnevale* week he and his father would rise at 2 A.M., milk the cows, then harness the cow, or the ox, the mule, or the donkey to get ready to work the land. They'd eat breakfast and set out at four for their two-hour walk to the field. At the end of the day, he still had the energy to dance and have fun. After the long walk home, he said, he found something to eat waiting for him, washed up, and went to dance until four in the morning. A half-hour of sleep, then back to work. "It was a hell of a life but I am sorry those days are gone," he said.

We sat on the good couch in Rita's mother's sitting room in her modern apartment. "It's not like today. Life is more tiring and people are more peevish," Rita's mother said. Husbands and wives used to dance. They ate cardoons and fava beans boiled with wild greens, and drank wine. "Now we don't lack either money or food," Rita's mother said, "but there is not the merry-making there was then."

The Feast of Saint Joseph was coming up on March 19, the anniversary of the day Mancuso met his bride. On that day years before, he had risen at four, taken the donkey to gather wood in the forest, come home, unloaded, washed, and gone to church. "There I found my *fidanzata.*" He simply laid eyes on the girl and instantly chose her for his wife. They could not talk. He could only see her face, and the smallest, smallest gesture of acceptance. Anything more would have made people gossip. Thus he entered the ornate rituals of peasant courtship. He went home and told his father he wanted to marry that girl. His father had to go see her father about it. A girl's father would always say, "Give me eight days' time; we need to talk about it at home," to make the suitor believe she was not interested.

So the two men met later. "Things can move ahead," the girl's father said. On Sunday, Mancuso and his parents paid a visit to the girl's cave. Signore Mancuso recounted and reen-acted the formal encounter:

"May we?"

"Please come in."

"Honor, it's an honor."

"So much honor to have you."

After a little chat, the girl's father said to his wife, "Call Caterina." When the girl made her entrance, all the men stood up, sat down, and repeated the stilted greetings. "We are honored, so honored." Then they got down to business: "My daughter would like your son." To seal the deal, she gave her hand. There was no kiss. The girl sat with her parents, sepa-rate from the boy. Every evening after that up until the wed-ding, Mancuso and his parents went to the girl's house; the gestures and the words never changed.

They married and made babies in a cave of their own, and danced together at *Carnevale*. Their lives were like the water in the stone—heated, crackling, and flowing through the veins of the cliff face.

30

GERACI SICULO

❧

I wanted to see the Sicily my grandparents never saw. I wanted lofty towns with narrow streets, fountains, a welcoming face, some feeling from the stone. Geraci Siculo was one of my best finds.

Geraci perches 3,534 feet up on a ridge between two peaks in the Madonie Mountains just twenty miles northeast of Polizzi Generosa. Its name probably derives from the Latin *jerax*, meaning "vulture's nest," and it was once the impenetrable seat of the Ventimiglia family, feudal marquises who owned the town from 1252 on. In 1454 the Ventimiglias moved to Castelbuono and let their Geraci castle go to ruins. Its broken ramparts look down over deep, wide valleys dotted with black Sicilian cattle. From the fortress ruins, I could see the hills below rear up like tidal waves.

The town center is so perfect it seems fake. Here is no asphalt or cement, only stone, sky, and water; there are fountains, cafés, and wooden church doors with pointed Arab arches. The most beautiful houses have walls of blue stones pieced together like a jigsaw puzzle, left exposed and unadorned. The begonias and nasturtiums trailing from the balconies form a flowered canopy over the steep stone-clad streets, which run vertically to the town's summit. They have archetypal names like Via Luna, Via Neve, and Cortile del Sole (Moon Street, Snow Street, and Sun Court). Older people zigzag uphill; kids in blue school smocks skip; some people lope. No one gets married in Geraci in the winter because if it snowed, no one could get to the church.

One reason Geraci is a favorite of mine is its abundance of sleek brown mules and the tough old farmers who ride them, a disappearing sight in Sicily. They gather at eight every morning at the fourteenth-century Fountain of the Most Holy Trinity where five gargoyles spew water into a forty-foot-long trough. The mules gulp the water, then plod down the road, dogs at their heels, farmers astride, headed to hillside vegetable patches.

In summer Geraci's population of 2,275 doubles with returning emigrants on vacation and city dwellers who come to see the world from on high, to breathe the mountain air and drink the local water. Geraci spring water, recommended for babies, is bottled at a town-owned plant and sold in drugstores throughout Italy. The same streams that fill the bottles also water the pocket rose gardens found all over town. Spotless as a Swiss village, Geraci pays a crew of unemployed twenty-somethings to clean the streets and water the roses. In the summer, the town hosts medieval jousts and a falconry contest.

I'd been to Geraci by bus often and had always stayed in a *pensione* or the stone-and-timber Hotel Ventimiglia. This time I found a ride with Giovanni, a Polizzi butcher, who was engaged to Rita, a Geraci girl who was studying for a doctorate in theology. On Wednesdays and Sundays he took the forty-minute ride to pick her up. He dropped me off in the piazza.

To increase rural tourism, the government of the *regione* of Sicily occasionally offers grants to homeowners willing to take in travelers. People use the money to remodel, upgrade their plumbing, add on rooms, pave the driveway, and fix the roof. They take in guests for a few years, then close to the public. All of the ten *pensioni* that had been in operation five years before had gone out of business, but I'd heard in Polizzi that an order of nuns here took in paying guests.

It was afternoon siesta time and the streets were deserted. I asked a lone woman in a black shawl to direct me to the convent, and she sent me to the cloistered Benedictines. I pulled my wheeled overnight case up stone staircases and steep alleys to the five-hundred-year-old convent. A woman at the entrance took me through its outer door then an inner one and left me in a vestibule. I rang a bell, sat down, and stared at an iron grate across a closed cupboard. A woman's voice came from behind it: "May Christ be praised." Not knowing the proper response, I said, *"Buon giorno."*

The cupboard opened and an aged nun in a familiar black habit stood behind the bars. I had spent thirteen years in

Catholic schools run by no-nonsense Benedictine nuns, so I braced myself.

"Who are you?" she asked.

I told her. She fingered her rosary behind her scapula as the interrogation began.

"Where are you from? . . . Do you have relatives here? . . . Are you traveling alone? . . . Where is your husband? . . . You're not married? . . . Do you have brothers? . . . How old are you? . . . Ohh! You look twenty-five. Is your father alive?"

Then: "What's that?" She pointed with her chin to my small suitcase.

"That is my suitcase."

"What is in it?"

"My clothes."

"How did you get here?"

"I came here with Giovanni the butcher from Polizzi." She raised her eyebrows. "He's engaged to Rita, from Geraci." Thank God she knew Rita. "Can you rent me a room?"

"No, we can't," she said. "We are cloistered."

I was disappointed. "I was told in Polizzi that you could."

"Whom do you know in Polizzi?"

"The Riccobene sisters," those pious twins, my ace in the hole.

"*Ahh, le farmaciste!* I'll call the superior."

Mother Superior arrived. More third degree.

"Why did you come to Geraci?" she asked.

"It's beautiful."

"Are you married? . . . How old are you? . . . Do you have children? . . . Are you Italian?"

"My paternal grandparents were Sicilians who emigrated to America. I studied Italian in Sicily."

"It's a good thing you speak Italian, or else what's the use of coming to Geraci?" she said, and disappeared through an inner door. She returned with two rock-hard almond cookies, the kind so sweet they make your teeth ache and your throat constrict. I thanked her and wrapped them in a napkin, intending to add them, further petrified, to my collection of odd Sicilian souvenirs.

"Why aren't you eating the cookies?" she asked.

"Because I am talking with you." It was true; I couldn't eat the cookies and talk. But to be polite, I bit off a chunk and chewed. Right away, she asked me another question. A crumb caught in my throat when I tried to answer. I coughed violently. Mother Superior smiled when I doubled over to dislodge it, a pretty sight.

"When you choke, think of us," she said.

Was that a curse or just some old saying? When I recovered I asked about them, since we had become so intimate. The nun who had greeted me was born in Geraci and had been cloistered here for fifty years, as was the superior, who was from Gangi, a nearby Madonie Mountain town. They introduced me to a third nun who had appeared behind the grate to see what all the fuss was about. She was about forty-five, "the youngest of us all," the superior said. Her face was serene, with a soap-and-water complexion, and for a split second I envied her. Life was a frothing stream for me but to them it was a quiet lake fed with prayer and meditation seeping up from the lake bed. I tried to imagine what I could do, what I would be, with a whole life spent facing inward.

"There are only seven of us left," Mother Superior said.

The doorbell rang. "May Christ be praised!" A woman answered, "Praised be His name." The superior nodded and the first nun buzzed her in, a woman with two eight-year-old girls. The superior told the girls to accompany me to the *collegio*, where nuns of the Collegiana Sisters order did indeed rent rooms to unmarried foreign women traveling alone in the mountains of Sicily.

The girls took me to Sister Geltrude, their catechism teacher, who prepared them to receive First Communion. We walked downhill past the town hall and halfway up the next steep rise, me huffing, the girls chattering. They said they had learned in school that the United States of America is a monarchy under Queen Elizabeth. "Have you ever seen the queen?" they wanted to know. I could not dissuade them. Across the piazza from the *chiesa madre* (Church of the Mother) a fountain spouted two icy streams. "If you're thirsty, you can drink," the girls said, and leaned over the fountain bowl to catch the stream between their lips. We turned right here. The girls brought me to a rude wooden door set in chunks of blue-gray stone and rang the buzzer.

Sister Geltrude dismissed the girls and turned to me. Maybe the Mother Superior had called ahead, or maybe

Sister Geltrude simply saw I wore no wedding ring, because the first thing she said to me was "You're not married?"

"No."

I carried my bag up a steep flight of steps. We came to a landing.

"Never married?"

"No."

"How old are you?"

"Forty-seven." A moment of silence.

"It is obvious that marriage was not your vocation." She took me to my room. Private bath, gas heater, electric bed warmer, and two twin beds. I was to pick one and sleep in it. A sign on the bedspread said, "Do not sit on this bed."

"You break the wires," Sister Geltrude explained. "Sit on the chair." She promised to plug in the bed warmer for me before I went to bed. A draft blew in through the leaky window guarded by a goose-breast fender made for peering into the street unseen. On the desk a glass was overturned on a green glass bottle of Geraci Siculo water. Next to it lay a soft leather-bound New Testament, well thumbed, printed on tissue paper in a microscopic type. Sister Geltrude advised me to be back from supper by ten, when she would lock the doors. "We get up at six, you know," she said, then left. Alone at last I riffled through the Good News and it opened to the Transfiguration, my favorite part, where Christ lifted off the ground and glowed.

My room was in a 262-year-old convent of the Collegio di Maria, run by the Collegiana Sisters since its founding by the

Geraci priest Don Gaetano Viviano as a school for local girls. Local volunteers built it with stones they hauled down from the mountains and sand they carted up from the beach at Cefalù. Don Viviano took two girls from town who volunteered to study to take the veil at a convent in Monreale, near Palermo. When the young women returned three years and nine months later, they found the *collegio* built and themselves named the two superiors. They taught the mountain girls to read and schooled them in the womanly arts of knitting, embroidery, sewing, and housekeeping. A girl of any social stratum could graduate and get a position as a teacher but the school's main purpose was to get the girls off the street and "prepare them to be good mothers and wives able to keep a nice home for the joy and serenity of all," according to a pamphlet Sister Geltrude gave me. The school closed in 1987 "because of the low birth rate." Now only three sisters remain in the adjoining convent, but the *collegio* is still open for catechism classes and for travelers "who want to spend days of meditation and prayer."

I went to the bar across the street, where seven men were playing cards. I had heard in Blufi that an American woman had settled in Geraci with her Sicilian husband, and I wanted to meet her. At the bar I asked about her.

"She lives in this very street and not a block from the piazza," one man said. He took me to her door and buzzed. Melissa Gay Rose came to the door and invited me in to her family's cliffside apartment. She folded me into her family life with no formalities or malaise. We were sister American adventurers in Sicily and we were glad to have found each other. Melissa was thirty-seven.

Her husband, Bruno, was out. I sat down and colored at the kitchen table with her daughters, known as Sissy and Earthquake, seven and five years old. The girls conversed with me in Italian but also spoke American English with British words thrown in. Melissa gave me tea and honey, then Bruno came home and we made dinner. I helped give the girls their baths and put them in their pajamas, then their mother read them a story in bed. Back in the kitchen Melissa broke out the cognac, then the grappa, hot and white, then the story of her own reception in Geraci.

Melissa Gay Rose grew up on a farm in Mississippi and became a dancer and contortionist. She was performing on the road in *A Chorus Line* when a girlfriend said to her, "Let's go to England," and they got on a plane. She had never even been in a train before, nor a taxi, nor handled foreign currency. At the airport in London, Melissa went to a phone booth and made hotel reservations; then the two of them went to a restaurant for dinner. Out of the kitchen walked Bruno Gargiulo, the owner, who eventually married Melissa Gay Rose. They started their family in London. When Melissa began to worry about her girls' safety on the city streets, they decided to move to the country, to Sicily, Bruno's homeland, where he had a brother and cousins in Palermo. Bruno sold the London restaurant and found some land for sale in Geraci Siculo, a town where they were both strangers. It was good farmland with a brook and views of the windblown mountains. They wanted to open an *agriturismo* in the old farm-house and serve food and wine they grew on their land.

From England they arranged to rent an apartment in the center of Geraci until they could get the farmhouse rebuilt. They packed up their London home, sent their belongings by freight, and drove to Sicily. Melissa knew she'd get here six weeks before her things arrived, so she packed several months' worth of life for four people in two suitcases, and that includ-ed clothes, shoes, sheets, blankets, pillows, pots, and four dish-es. They drove for twenty-four hours, "and then we started our new life."

It started badly. The man who had rented them the apart-ment over the phone had since sold the place, but told the family they could stay in his attic. Melissa and Bruno, both five feet ten, kept hitting their heads on the ceiling. It was winter and there was no heat, and not enough current to run the lights and the water pump at the same time. "I had to wash dishes in the dark," Melissa said. The third night they were there, in the worst wind and rainstorm anyone can remember ("All the trees died," Melissa said), Earthquake fell out of her top bunk and her tooth pierced her upper lip. She'd sustained a concussion and had to spend two days in the hospital. But it didn't end there: Earthquake's second scar was in her eyebrow, from a fall off a six-foot cliff. Third scar: a burn on the inside of her legs from stinging jelly fish at the beach.

After just six weeks, the girls were fluent in Italian and had been enrolled in the public elementary school. Despite the utter strangeness of having foreigners live in the center of town, the townspeople made Melissa feel welcome, she said. And Melissa began to make her mark on Geraci.

"My own nickname is Tornado." She shook up Geraci when, unbidden and unpaid, Melissa made new curtains for the school's disused stage. The school had phased out its arts curriculum six years before, and now she started recycling to obtain materials to be used for art projects and dazzled the townspeople with American-style ideas. At Christmas she and Sissy's classmates covered the school in silver foil made from potato-chip snack bags turned inside out. Now Sissy's school decorates for all the American holidays—Saint Patrick's Day, Valentine's Day, the Fourth of July. "It makes Sissy feel special," she said.

The people were amazed. At first they couldn't fathom Melissa's motives—after all, no one was paying her. "There is no parental volunteerism here," Melissa said. But then she gave a speech at school urging parents to have fun with their kids, and now six other mothers volunteer. Before long, the students had three art shows going, and their stage had a new curtain.

In return, Melissa now has peace of mind. Sissy and Earthquake can play outside all day and Melissa never worries about them. She knows they will be fed and looked after wherever they are. "In Sicily, you cannot go to somebody's house without being invited in for tea and biscuits. As soon as you get ready to go they beg you to stay five minutes more," she said. "I was received warmly in this town."

It was getting late, I had to go. Melissa begged me to stay five minutes more but I explained about my curfew. I walked the ten feet back to the convent and crawled into my pre-warmed bed. Sister Geltrude let herself in to extinguish the gas heater and to tell me good night. "Dreams of gold," she said, and clicked off the light.

31

FREEDOM

ॐ

One thing distinguishes Polizzi Generosa from most other mountain towns: for the better part of its 2,300 years of recorded history, Polizzi belonged only to kings. Its citizens were free of the tyranny and taxes imposed by lesser nobles and enjoyed the sovereign's personal protection. Kings wanted this town for its strategic position at the fork of two valleys; its life-giving streams and rivers, mountain forests, fertile land, and bracing air; and its shiplike rock, made to rule from. The town in turn wanted kings for their patronage. Polizzi's natural gifts made her rich. Her wealth bought her freedom; this freedom spawned a special breed of people who even today still give their first fruits to neighbors. Celestina Salamone, the town historian, said, "We are generous because we have always been free."

The history of Polizzi is a microcosm of the history of the mountain towns of Sicily's interior. Twenty years ago, in the weeds off a road that descends from the arches of Polizzi's fifteenth-century aqueduct, two friends of mine, Santo LiPani and Moffo Schimmenti, a restaurateur and a farmer, found the Fonte Naftolia, the Thalia Fountain, a rudely carved stone in the shape of the nymph Thalia. According to local myth, Thalia mated with the volcano god Adrano deep in Etna's womb, then bore the twins Castor and Pollux, the Palici gods. The pudgy stone nymph Thalia once spewed water through the O of her lips into a wide, welcoming bowl formed by her lower body.

In the third century B.C. a colony of Greeks settled in Polizzi and made roof tiles and fine vases from the abundant clay deposits that are still mined there today. In 1938, in the heart of the town, archaeologists found coins and terra-cotta objects giving evidence of Greek settlement and contact with Carthage. The three-faced statue of the Egyptian goddess Isis was found hidden in a well in the same street.

As a string of conquerors sent cultural shockwaves through the island, Sicilians rolled with the punches. When Rome conquered Greece, Sicilians spoke Latin. When Rome fell to barbarian tribes, the Greek Orthodox patriarch took the place of the pope, and Sicilians spoke Greek. When the Arabs fought to settle the Madonie Mountains in the mid–ninth century they were met by the walls of Basileapolis, the newly founded "city of the king," the Byzantine ruler, on the hill where Polizzi now rises. In A.D. 882 the Arabs defeated Byzantine forces in a field near Polizzi. The Arab general sent three thousand severed heads on pikes to Palermo as cautionary trophies of war. Sicilians began to speak Arabic.

Denis Mack Smith wrote in his *A History of Sicily: Medieval Sicily 800–1713*, that wherever Arabs met resistance they killed all the men and sent the prettiest women and boys to the *khalif*, their ruler, or to the slave auction block. People in towns that surrendered were allowed to practice their religions and to repair churches and synagogues but not to build new ones. Christians and Jews had to place distinguishing marks on their clothing and homes, had to yield to Muslims in the roadway, rise when a Muslim entered the room, and pay higher taxes than the conquering Arabs—which discouraged Muslims from trying to convert them. Christians couldn't carry arms, ride horseback, saddle their mules, ring their church bells, carry the crucifix in procession, drink wine in public, or read the Bible within earshot of a Muslim, Denis Mack Smith wrote. "All this was harsh, but it hardly amounted to religious persecution."

In Polizzi the Greek Orthodox gathered in a neighborhood around the Church of San Pancrazio. The Sephardic Jews had their synagogue, baths, and pharmacies near what is now Via Carlo V. The Arabs' mosque was in the present Church of Saint Antonio Abate, converted to a Christian church in 1361 but still topped by an onion dome.

One winter morning I sat hunched on a cold stone bench in the sun in Piazza Gramsci, near some men wearing woolen hooded capes. Signora Salamone, Polizzi's historian, waved to me from her balcony and beckoned me up.

"Here again?" She knew Polizzi kept drawing me back. "You like Polizzi because we are cosmopolitan," she said,

meaning cosmopolitan in its true sense: world-wise, not limit-
ed to the local.

Celestina Salamone was now in her eighties. She had written three books on Polizzi's history and was working on the
fourth, about its dialect. As a girl she had learned to converse
in Latin and Greek; she could read French, German, and
English, and now she was teaching herself Arabic. She said
most of the Sicilian names for springs, fountains, and watering
holes have Arabic roots. For example, a copious fountain once
gushed in Polizzi's Via Garraffo, so named because *gharaf* in
Arabic means "abundant in water." *Ayn* was Arabic for spring
water, and *fuhara,* for water that danced impetuously from its
source. In the ninth century, the Sicilian-Arab geographer
Edrusi described his trip to Polizzi as "a most beautiful sojourn."
To the people of the desert, Sicily was the Garden of Eden.

Half a million Muslims from Africa and Spain settled
Orthodox Greek Sicily in the ninth and tenth centuries,
when forests and streams abounded and the rivers were still
navigable. "The Arabs were drawn here by the water,"
Celestina Salamone said. Their wise men were geographers,
astronomers, mathematicians, poets, translators, and hy-
draulic engineers, and their farmers were robust, hardworking
settlers who learned to live beside the resident Greek-speak-
ing population.

Consequently, when the Normans came in the eleventh
century, Roger I, count of Sicily (1031–1101), found the people
of Polizzi already "less rough-hewn, a little more civilized,"
Signora Salamone said. Roger de Hauteville (Ruggero in

Italian), was one of six sons of Tancred de Hauteville who were French-speaking Norman mercenaries with a genius for warfare and administration. They pillaged their way to fortunes in southern Italy and Sicily and built a dynasty on their booty. The de Hautevilles were nominally Roman Catholics, although they did not seem overly religious. According to Denis Mack Smith, Pope Nicholas II, in order to regain land for the Roman Catholic church, in 1059 authorized a Norman nobleman, Robert Guiscard, and his youngest brother, Roger de Hauteville, "to govern as much of southern Italy as they could conquer, and Guiscard in return agreed not to recognize the religious authority of Constantinople." Guiscard established papal fiefs in Apulia, but he decided to rule Sicily on his own if he could take it. He put his brother in charge of conquering the island, which Roger took from a main base in the heartland mountains. From his headquarters in Troina, he campaigned in the Madonie and nearby Nebrodi Mountains, capturing and rebuilding Arab forts in Polizzi, Petralia, Sperlinga, Gangi, and Geraci. By 1091, Noto, a southern city that was the last Muslim stronghold in Sicily, had fallen to the Normans.

Under the Normans, Muslims and Jews had to pay a special tax, but Arabs, Jews, and Greek Orthodox alike were allowed freedom of culture and religion. Greek and Arabic continued to be used alongside French and Latin in the Normans' court. The same kind of melting pot that later made America great produced Sicily's Golden Age.

Count Roger declared Polizzi part of his personal estate and built the town's principal church, dedicated to Most Holy

Mary Assumed into Heaven, in 1085. "Remember, this is the king's church. Care for it well," he is supposed to have said one time as he departed from the city. It remained a bishop's seat throughout the 1700's and still stands today. Roger's granddaughter, Countess Adelasia of Polizzi, built up Polizzi at a time when it hosted populations speaking Greek, Arabic, Latin, and Hebrew. The city's ethnic neighborhoods were called *capitanea*, for each was headed by a captain, and each one had its own piazza, place of worship, system of justice, and public fountain. Interneighborhood marriages were forbidden.

Polizzi prospered, propelled by water, the creator of wealth. Melted snow gushed from rocks, watered the fields, turned the mill wheels, and filled the rivers that carried grain and goods to seaport markets. The first gristmill was built in 1067. Polizzi's cool mountain air, spring water, and majestic panoramas drew royal visitors and their cultural entourages: Queen Elizabeth of Aragon and her son, Ludovico, who in 1342 at the age of five became king of Trinacria (Sicily); Queen Mary, the wife of King Martin the Young, who died in 1390; Queen Bianca of Navarre, viceroy of the kingdom of Sicily in the 1400's; and the Holy Roman emperor Charles V, who stopped on his way back from Tunisia in 1535 and stayed at the house of the local nobleman GianBartolo LaFarina.

Polizzi shone brightest during the Renaissance, when it was the meeting point for the two most important grain highways in Sicily. The two upper branches of the Imera River met here: the Fiume Grande (Big River) and the Xireni (or Lower Imera). The royal grain road followed the river, flanked on both sides by fields of wheat and other cereals, another wide, nourishing bowl. Whoever controlled the grain road was rich. In the fifteenth and sixteenth centuries the wealthy and noble families of Pisa, Genoa, Catalan, France, and the Arab world built homes in Polizzi and took control of the valleys.

Here the firstborn son inherited his father's title and estate; his younger brothers became learned clergymen, crusaders, or knights-errant. His sisters married as well as they could or became nuns. Polizzi's monasteries and convents flourished in number and wealth. Some were established for less than pious reasons. For example, the Badia Nuova, or "new abbey," is a former Benedictine convent so named to distinguish it from the old abbey, the Badia Vecchia. The Badia Nuova was built in 1499 by the powerful Signorino family to console poor Sister Scholastica, their daughter, for not having been elected abbess of the Badia Vecchia. Founding a new convent was a show of power; Scholastica Signorino staffed the Badia Nuova and ran it her way.

As the town grew in wealth, its generosity increased. In Polizzi the rotating shelf in the orphanage wall was called the Holy Wheel, and members of the middle class helped support the babies found on it. Lords gave dowries to poor girls so they could marry. And every Friday it was the custom of noble ladies to stand at their gates offering alms to mendicants.

You can tell much about a town by its heroes and heroines, even the legendary ones. Donna Laura, says Polizzi's historian, Signora Salamone, was a sixteenth-century noblewoman, a daughter of the Ventimiglia family of Geraci Siculo and Castelbuono. "She was beautiful, good, pious, and rich," Signora Salamone said. She came to Polizzi to marry the son of the man who had hosted Emperor Charles V, GianBartolo LaFarina. Donna Laura was generous to all and was the most humble mother of two sons, who were killed by the plague in the mid–1500's. The people loved her and gave her name to a stone watertower so that no one would forget her. "Her spirit is in the stone."

The town's churches multiplied until at one point there were more than a hundred, and its abbeys filled with books and works of art. Cultural life thrived. In the Middle Ages Polizzi had hospitals, public fountains, seminaries, and hostels for pilgrims. The first public laws, published on parchment in the 1300's, established the last call at taverns, prohibited the clandestine killing of bulls, and forbade taking stones from the roadbed. The first public clock was installed on the façade of the chiesa madre in 1406, soon after clocks were invented. The first aqueduct, built in 1476, provided free irrigation for all inhabitants' fields. In 1572 the Jesuits started a school of "First Letters" which they later expanded to offer university-level studies. In 1901 one of the gristmills was modified into a hydroelectric plant that gave Polizzi electric streetlights when even the coastal cities were still using gas lamps.

From the ninth century through the Renaissance, Polizzi was a center of learning, much of it carried on by numerous religious orders: the Jesuits, Dominicans, Franciscans, the Observants, Conventual, Fatebenefratelli, the Sovereign

Military Order of Malta, the Teutonic Knights, the Order of the Preaching Brothers, the Regular Third Order of Saint Francis of Assisi, the Capuchin and Carmelite brothers, the Franciscan Missionaries of Baby Jesus, and several contingents of Benedictine nuns were represented. German priests who answered directly to Rome staffed one thirteenth-century church in Piazza Trinità. (The church is now an apartment building with an altar in the ground-floor ceramic shop.)

Here, the monks and nuns and members of the clergy were most often the learned sons and daughters of noble or wealthy Polizzi families. They copied manuscripts, made translations, wrote screeds, illustrated and bound books, and ran hospitals, schools, and hostels.

ॐ   ॐ   ॐ

In 1866, Polizzi profited enormously from a federal law passed by a newly unified Italy whereby all religious property—lands, convents, abbeys, hospitals, art, furniture, and books—was turned over to the towns. The local library inherited a treasure.

One morning Graziella Ortolano, the librarian, took me on a tour of the recently restored Duca Lancia di Brolo Library. We walked up three flights of shallow twelve-foot-wide steps. "This used to be the Jesuit convent," Graziella said. "They say they wanted the stairs this broad so the priests could ride their horses up them three abreast." Girolamo Mistretta, a Jesuit nobleman from Polizzi, paid for the construction of the dwelling and attached school, which took seventy years to build. He never saw it finished.

She took me to an inner room where the temperature and humidity were controlled to see dozens of precious incunabula—books from 1450 to 1500, the "cradle" period of printing (the Latin *incunabula* refers to bands holding a baby in a cradle). "The Gutenberg press was invented in the first half of the fourteen hundreds," she reminded me as she opened a treatise on the meaning of Lent, printed in Venice in 1487. It had no frontispiece, but instead, an *ochiello*, "a little eye," with the book's title, the author's name, and the words "Laus Deo." Praise God. Surrounding the printed text were finely penned miniature figures that were hand-colored and gilded. An Arab numeral appeared at the top of every page and a Latin letter at the bottom. "We have forty-five of these restored incunabula," Graziella said. She closed the book and showed me the binding. "Sheepskin. You can see the hairs."

In the 1500's books were unbound pages stacked between parchment covers. I was shocked to see that someone had scribbled numbers in pencil all over one of these covers. Graziella said the culprit was probably the original owner, who needed something to write on at the time. "There was no paper," she said. Handwritten comments appeared in the margins and a tiny braceleted hand pointed to salient points in the Latin text—"a medieval highlighter," Graziella said. She handed me another book, a list of the noble Sicilian families of Polizzi. I looked up Marco Galliano's name: "Noble family of Norman origin, already present in Polizzi at the end of the fifteenth century. This branch is probably from Naples, some say Padua." The first Galliano built a house here in 1504, it said, then listed the brothers who followed him, the location of their family chapel and burial ground, and their coat of arms, a lion rampant surrounded by seven seashells on a field of blue.

It was dark when I walked back to the inn. Orange lights warmed the walls of the castle, the chiesa madre, the convents, courtyards, *collegio*, and abbeys, dreamlike in the perpetual mist. The quiet was elevating. I could hear my soles slapping on the stones; in some streets they even made an echo.

ℤ→ ℤ→ ℤ→

About seven one morning, in the calm after an all-night storm, I heard the church bells ring just four times. When Signora Albanese invited me to her kitchen for coffee I asked her what the bells meant.

"Did you count the strokes?" she asked. "It was three or four."

"They tolled four times."

"It was the *agonia*," she said. "Someone died in the night. Three times for a man, four times for a woman." In the town of Collesano, they call it *il terminale*. In Polizzi, she told me, whoever hears the bells says, "I hope it didn't harm the family"— exressing the hope that it was an old person who died, not someone young. "This is our custom."

Francesco, who worked with the Riccobene sisters, knew I was interested in these small-town traditions that give dignity to life. "Do you know about *il bando?*" he asked me one day as he drove me to Locati.

"No, what is it?"

"Thirty years ago, if you lost a lamb or a kid from your flock, you could hire a man who would walk through the streets of Polizzi playing his trumpet and shouting, 'Whoever has found a stray lamb, please report it to X, the rightful owner.' " And in this town the lamb, if found, would be returned.

"The sheer height of the mountains" shaped Polizzi's character, Celestina Salamone said. The high country attracted people with independent minds, who realized that they must respect the odd beliefs of others if they wished to live in peace themselves. "This is tolerance," she said. "Generosity is not only putting a coin in someone's hand. It is allowing freedom of thought. Each for his own dignity, be it the Bible or the Koran."

I'd seen this practical virtue in action in Polizzi. Once I was a passenger in my friend Santo's car when he stopped, blocking traffic, to chat with a friend. They must have talked for eight minutes. Ten cars backed up behind us, clogging entry to the Corso Garibaldi. No one beeped or said a word in a situation that would have caused road rage in Palermo. I mentioned this to Santo when he finally tooled off.

He said, "They don't beep because they know that next time it's their turn."

32

WITHOUT A MAN

❦

ONE DAY IN POLIZZI I sat on a blue stool in Enza Dolce's nameless store next to an empty ice cream freezer. She was thirty-eight, single, thin as a rail, with black hair and almond-shaped eyes. She had just returned from her winter job in Tuscany, where she glued abrasive pads onto sponges at her brother-in-law's factory. We'd met the year before. She lived with her mother and owned this store where she sold soda, chewing gum, potato chips, juice, cocktails, and espresso. In the summer she was famous for her homemade gelato. But this was late March; Piazza Trinità was deserted, and Enza was depressed.

I was to learn that Polizzi's tolerance does not necessarily extend to Sicilian women. "Some people here don't like the fact that I've made it this far without a man," she said.

She had just had another run-in with a neighbor who claimed the parking space that she used beside her store was his private territory, and he demanded she move her car. He said he needed it empty for easy access to his garage. Enza knew the laws and claimed the space was public property. The appropriate town stamp did not appear on her neighbor's store-bought "No Parking" sign, and furthermore she never blocked access to his garage. That evening he'd entered the store, nodded at me, turned to Enza where she sat on her stool behind the counter, and yelled insanely in dialect for twenty seconds, then left.

"At least he was brief," I said when he was gone.

"Brief and very concise," Enza said. "Did you hear what he said? He'd have my hide. That means kill me." The threat seemed excessive for a dispute about a parking spot; this battle of wills had been escalating for years. With no man to champion her, Enza was easy prey. Someone had slashed three tires and had scratched the paint on her car.

Enza took the threats and verbal abuse. She could leave Polizzi and stay in the north, where she had sisters, "but I love the stones here," she said. She could just give in and park elsewhere, but parking wasn't the point. "The point is that the man must win over the woman," she said, and this one wanted her store closed. Enza drew a line and wouldn't budge.

I admired her. I was a little like her. We had both tasted the pleasures of autonomy—making plans and carrying them out. She was ambitious, quick-witted, independent, tenacious, hardworking, and thrifty, a wonderful mix for a man but a volatile combination for a woman in a small Sicilian town. Her gifts marginalized her.

My friends the Riccobene sisters, unmarried twins who run a pharmacy in Locati, twenty minutes from Polizzi, ran into similar problems. Independent, unmarried, childless women like Enza, Rosaria, and Antonietta are rare birds in Sicily. They all say it irks some Sicilian men to see them succeed. Maybe their discomfort is the reaction of insecure men to proof that they are not indispensable.

Most Sicilian country women don't have to contend with such problems because they'd never find themselves in Enza's situation. I know plenty who seem to live happily with clipped wings. For fleeting moments I've envied their safe, ordered, socially approved lives. Most Sicilian country girls grow up in patriarchal families, learn to clean, go to grammar school and high school, fill their hope chests with cutwork linens, marry suitably, have children, attend Sunday Mass, keep house, and stay at home. Those who work outside the home have the permission and protection of a father, husband, or son. But this was not Enza's fate.

Her father had died when she was a toddler, leaving seven children fatherless. From age two to eleven she was raised by Franciscan nuns in a Polizzi *collegio* similar to the one in nearby Geraci Siculo. For Enza, Polizzi's Collegio di Maria was a poor child's nightmare. At the time of her father's death, the roof was off their house in preparation for an expansion, and her mother, Peppina, had no money to pay the workers. She sent the two oldest girls, who were thirteen and fourteen, to Germany, to work and send back money to finish the house. She sent three of the younger girls, including Enza, to the Collegio di Maria in the center of Polizzi, where the Region of Sicily paid the Franciscan nuns to feed and educate her children. Some of the students were paying boarders; others, like Enza and her sisters, were state-subsidized orphans. After five years, Enza's older sisters went to work in Germany too and left the seven-year-old to fend for herself in the convent.

Her mother was not allowed to visit the orphanage; it would have been too disruptive. If on Sunday Enza turned around in church to search out her mother's eyes, the nuns punished her for disobedience. Students who paid tuition were allowed to have long hair, but the nuns gave the orphan girls a military buzz cut. They said they did it in the name of hygiene, but the paying girls did not have to submit; for Enza, a shaved head was mortification. "Maybe they did it to cut down on the electric bill." She had to bathe with other girls and keep her underwear on. They made her eat food she hated. Once the nuns locked her in the dining room for ten hours in front of a plate of polenta because she had refused to eat it.

The nuns taught her to read, do sums, and keep house and to sew, embroider, crochet, knit, do cutwork, and make lace. "When I made a mistake, instead of showing me the right way, the nun would poke my hand with a needle," Enza said. Enza had none of her childhood works in her hope chest because the nuns bought them for pennies, then sold them at a profit.

The mother superior put Enza's meager earnings in the child's piggy bank, but once a year she collected all the girls' banks to pay for their dues in a Catholic youth league, for which they received a paper certificate of membership in return.

One of Enza's friends wet the bed at night, but instead of sending her to a doctor, the nuns made her wear her underwear on her head as a punishment, Enza said. "The nuns were bitter women who took out their own frustrations on those weaker than them," she said. While they were teaching her that the weak must submit, Enza was making other plans.

When she was eleven her mother was finally able to bring her home. The first thing she did was to grow her hair long. At eleven she sold Avon products door to door. At twelve she went to work for a tailor who paid her five thousand lire a week. Polizzi once had many tailors, one of whom was the father of the designer Domenico Dolce, of Dolce e Gabbana. Enza said the designer was ostracized because he was gay, and when he left he vowed never to return. When the mayor later gave him the key to the city, Dolce sent a representative to collect it. (Polizzi is a fountainhead of talent; Martin Scorsese's father, Charles, was born here, too.) Enza saved for five years and was the first girl in Polizzi to own a motor scooter, which she paid for in cash. She had eclectic tastes in music and became the Madonie region's first woman deejay, broadcasting from a Polizzi disco inside what was once the writer Giovan Battista Caruso's house and drawing partiers from Palermo and Catania. Her mother screamed at her nightly for coming home late. Enza scandalized Polizzi by taking a job as a home health assistant, then considered too lowly a job for a woman of decent family. But she was saving for a dream: to own a business and be her own boss.

When she was twenty-seven Enza went deep into debt, flew to Parma to buy pasta machines, and opened her own fresh-pasta business in a rented storefront in Polizzi. The *chiesa e casa*—church and home—women's brigade insinuated that she must have sold her body to buy the machines. "People made bets about when my business would fold," she said. This hurt her. Enza had created her own job, harmed no one, paid for her permits, and offered a service to the public, but her neighbors reviled her. She couldn't sell enough pasta to stay in business. When she sold her equipment a truck came to pick it up. She told no one about the good deal she had struck with the buyer. "People stopped the driver on his way out of town and asked him how much I'd sold the machines for," Enza said. Before she left the store that day, she got down on her knees and prayed for something that would let her save face. For a while, the wags thought they'd won. But Enza took a night course to earn a business license and in a few weeks she opened her ice cream store in the same locale.

Most of her friends now are from out of town. She tries to ignore jealous criticism and live her honest life; she has a kind heart and will not let them change her. She remembers to put drops in her old widower landlord's eyes twice a day. She cleans the house of her best friend's widowed father, because her best friend married and moved to Germany. He gives her bunches of chicory in return.

Enza lives in town with her mother; they take care of each other. But Enza's dream is to retire at the small orchard house she has bought, three miles out of town and a world away from troublesome men.

33

THE SECRET SPRING

※

IT WAS TIME TO GO THROUGH THE CLOSETS at Nana's house in New Jersey. My two sisters and I each put aside what we wanted. I chose Papa's cane, his checkerboard, and odd, inscrutable inventions, Nana's wedding sheets, the patched black pocketbook with her last pay stub, her pots and pans, the arm-wide pasta bowl, the *Last Supper* above Papa's cot. But their real treasure was inside me. The last time I went to Sicily, it was winter and I stayed in the mountains.

"You can write at my house in Pietà Bassa," Enza said. Three years before, against her mother's wishes, she had bought the house and nut orchard three miles outside Polizzi.

The road to Lower Pity was paved with pink stones. Enza's white house perched squarely on a steep hill planted with diagonal rows of hazelnut trees. "The farm has only belonged to women," Enza said. She had acquired it from a ninety-year-old woman who had inherited it from her grandmother who got it from her mother. "I bought the place with what I made on the pasta machines," Enza said.

We sat on her back stoop and looked at her land. Hand-dug irrigation ditches ran among the trees. Strange orchids, their petals tipped with soft black fur, sprouted by the hundreds in the lush green grass. Tangled ropes of ivy draped the moss-covered rocks. Wild pink cyclamen grew in clumps near a brook that rang with melting snow. All around us the saw-toothed mountains stood white-capped, just as I used to draw mountains before I had ever seen them.

"Are you thirsty?" Enza asked. She filled a glass at the bathroom tap and brought it out to me. "It's the water of the Madonna," she said as I drank. It was from the stream that nourished her land, and it tasted like clarity itself. The fountainhead was just above the house. I decided to unpack and write.

I moved in and fell into my daily routine. I set up my laptop on her dining-room table, with books, maps, notes, and pens each in a pile of their own. Enza filled vases with black orchids, almond blossoms, and tiny pink cyclamen and lit the charcoal brazier that I set at my feet when I worked. I got up before dawn to write. When I opened the green shutters I saw the lights of Polizzi, still glittering in the dark. When the sun rose, sweet light filled the green valley. Birds sang in the thin gray hazelnut branches at the window. At noon I could hear bells ringing the Angelus three miles away.

Enza figured this would be her retirement home, after her mother died, since her mother, Peppina, wouldn't let her live here alone, for fear of thieves. But whenever Enza had house-guests she slept here. Peppina had washed and dried the shorn wool of nineteen sheep to stuff Enza's seven mattresses and twelve pillows. She had covered the beds and windows with matching white crocheted spreads. The burnt-orange valance in the living room had been cut from an old satin coverlet. Enza had unraveled her old sweaters to knit blankets and had braided rugs from strips of her worn-out T-shirts. She had planted roses, dahlias, pansies, angel trumpets, papyrus, prickly pears, Shasta daisies, parsley, fava beans, onions, lemons, cherries, and a weeping willow, her favorite tree. It helped her to dispel old sorrows.

In September she and her mother harvested her hazelnut crop. "They are not ripe until they fall from the branch, then each one must be picked up singly," Enza said. The profit from her nut crop was just enough to pay the man who plowed and pruned her orchard. She'd spent three years collecting rocks he turned up every spring and saved them to be used for foundation fill for a patio. Enza looked deceptively fragile but she was deep-rooted, single-minded and resistant—shades of my Nana, who was made on another Sicilian hill.

Moffo's farm was just up the street. He was a "farmer by choice," one who had studied and could have done other things but chose to work the land. He and Enza had been friends since she left the convent at age eleven. "How long do hazelnut trees live?" I asked him when he came to lend her his wheelbarrow.

"Centuries!" Moffo said.

They looked too delicate. "You mean each tree?" I asked.

"Not each tree, but each new trunk grows from the same root," Moffo said. "There have been hazelnuts on this hillside since the Arabs."

๛ ๛ ๛

Sometimes Enza would take me to town to have lunch with her mother. Their kitchen was three flights up and always smelled like Nana's. "Why are the kitchens always on the top floor?" I asked.

"Because people are nosy," Peppina said. The kitchen is the room most likely to be messy, so no one puts it on the ground floor where people can look in. Enza's favorite lunch was boiled chicory sautéed in garlic and mine was artichoke frittatas. Peppina could hardly stand for the pain in her legs, so when she wasn't cooking or cleaning she sat by the brazier in the light of her balcony door crocheting dizzying patterns with hair-thin white twine. "I can't sit still and do nothing," she said. I imagined she'd never had much chance with seven children and no husband.

"How did your husband die?" I asked.

"He had a stone that made it difficult to pass urine." His condition was painful but he was too embarrassed to stand naked before the doctor. "In those days it was different," she said. He'd had the pain since he was a teenager, and when he arrived at her door with his parents to ask for Peppina's hand, a neighbor lady leaned out her window and whispered, "Don't take him. He is not well." Peppina knew it but married him anyway. "I liked him," she said. Decades later, when he was finally operated on, doctors removed an egg-sized stone, but another one grew and finally killed him. Enza has no memory of her father.

Her hands were callused from churning handmade ice cream in the summer; she saved her money to build the patio. She hired her nephew to make the stone wall around it but she herself mixed the cement, hauling buckets of water and wheelbarrows of sand. All day as I wrote I heard the chink of rocks she pitched onto the fill pile. She would clean up her property and burn dead branches and debris. In the coals she roasted artichokes, then she boiled water to cook pasta, then she scraped the coals into the brazier and brought it inside so we wouldn't waste their heat.

Every evening she drove to town to open her snack store at *passeggiata* time. Some winter nights she'd make just five dollars, but she opened for business out of pride and stubbornness. She took a bottle of Madonna water with her to work.

One day I asked Enza to take me to the stream's source. To guide us she brought home an expert, Giuseppe Lavanco, a seventy-three-year-old retired plumber who knew every spring, source, and pipe in Polizzi. First he took us to the Madonna's spring; it was encased in cement. We stood there, disappointed, listening to its deep-throated gurgle. "There are others," said Lavanco, who was warming to this task. He knew of 106 springs that give a total of two thousand liters per second. "These mountains make water," he said. I wanted to see it flow fresh from the rock.

In a dell named Lower Holy Cross the water trickled into a man-made pond whose surface reflected the towering mountains where it was born. At Almond Flats a ten-foot waterfall thundered beside a doddering almond in full bloom. It made Lavanco mad: all that pure water bursting from years in the dark to flow untapped to the river then the sea. "Wasted!" he said. It could have been watering hazelnuts.

Then he took us to the Sorgente Capicelli, a tiny spring on private land. He parked the car on a ridge and we walked into a valley, our heels digging up the scent of moist soil, past an abandoned country church, through a hazelnut orchard, down a grassy bank, to a cushion of cyclamen perfumed with ferns. There a stream flowed clear from a fissure in the rock and laughed as it entered the light.

This was my blood, conceived deep in a Sicilian mountain. It knew how to flow with life. It nourished what it touched. It cut its own channel, found other streams, and flowed downhill to lap at other shores. I cupped my hand and drank at the source.

SELECTED BIBLIOGRAPHY

Barzini, Luigi. *The Italians*. New York: Bantam Books,1964.

Cristodaro, Celestina Salamone. *Polizzi Prenormanna; Il Silenzio Storico*. Palermo: l'Associazione Culturale THULE, 1998.

D'Amico, Renato, editor. *Catania; I Quartieri della Metropoli*. Catania: Le Nove Muse, 2000.

Dolci, Danilo. *Report from Palermo*. New York: Orion Press, 1959.

Farella, Flaviano D. *Stradario Storico di Polizzi Generosa*. Palermo: Fiamma Serafica, 1907.

Fava, Giuseppe. *I Siciliani*. Bologna: Nuova Casa Editrice L. Capelli, 1987.

Finley, M. I. *A History of Sicily: Ancient Sicily to the Arab Conquest*. New York: Viking, 1968.

Fucà, Raffaele. *Santuario Madonna dell'Olio: Appunti di Storia*. Palermo: Fiamma Serafica, 1977.

Goethe, Johann Wolfgang von. *Italian Journey*. New York: Penguin Books, 1970.

Hamilton, Edith. *Mythology: Timeless Tales of Gods and Heroes*. New York: Mentor, 1940.

Jung, Carl Gustav. *Man and His Symbols*. Garden City, N.Y.: Doubleday, 1964.

Lampedusa, Giuseppe di. *The Leopard*. Translated by Archibald Colquhoun. New York: Pantheon Books, 1960.

_____. *Two Stories and a Memory*. New York: Everyman's Library, 1991.

La Placa, Giuseppe. *Un Mondo Che Scompare: Nel Bacino dell'alto Salso*. Città di Petralia Soprana: 1994

La Rosa, Ugo, editor. *Guida della Sicilia e delle Isole Minori*. Palermo and Rome: Ugo La Rosa Editore, 1990.

Robb, Peter. *Midnight in Sicily*. New York: Vintage Departures, 1991.

Smith, Denis Mack. *A History of Sicily: Medieval Sicily 800–1713*. New York: Viking Press, 1968.